Congregational Paths to Holiness

Peter A.R. Stebinger

FORWARD MOVEMENT PUBLICATIONS
CINCINNATI, OHIO

®

©2000
Forward Movement Publications
412 Sycamore Street
Cincinnati, Ohio 45202 USA
www.forwardmovement.org

Contents

Introduction

William Tully's chapter in *Building Up The Church*, presented by Forward Movement Publications to the General Convention of 1997, begins with these words:

"If one thing above all was true of the first Christians and their fledgling churches, it was they were alive. After the darkness of the crucifixion and the mystery of the resurrection, the scattering uncertainty of Jesus' followers turned into a period of realization, powered by the Pentecost moment, that the Christ would live in what they came to call the Body of Christ.

"To be alive a body must grow. That is the law of all living things. Health and life depend on growth. There is no no-growth option."

Peter Stebinger's new book, *Congregational Paths to Holiness* is herewith presented to General Convention 2000 with the clear and demonstrable conviction that where and when those of us who are the Body of Christ gather and open themselves to the lively presence of the Spirit of God we are blessed with growth and new life.

Stebinger's story is exciting and hopeful, opening the way for congregations of many different varieties to "go and do likewise" by fostering a place and the promise of new life in the Spirit.

—Edward Stone Gleason
Editor

Preface

This work brings to the Church some exciting news about how, and why, some congregations grew during a period when most did not.

It emerges from an ongoing project. For 17 years I have been the rector of a healthy, mid-sized congregation in Connecticut. We serve two towns with a combined population of about 9,000. We are thriving. As one who has led this congregation for a long time, I always look for new ways to help us become stronger.

There are many diocesan parish development and mission strategies. Unfortunately, as the debate is inconclusive, the underlying strategy has often been inconsistent. In one place, the megachurch is held up as the model; in another, conservative theology is seen as the key; in a third, demographic change is viewed as the most important variable. The result is chaos. Different influences will affect different congregations in distinct ways. This knowledge should lead to different strategies for growth in different situations, but too often clergy and congregations are offered a "one-size-fits-all" strategy from a diocese.

I believe God will grant growth in numbers where we are serving well. I do not, however, believe the reverse is necessarily true-that where a congregation is shrinking the community is being poorly served-although this may be true in some cases.

I use a pseudonym for the diocese under study. Because an entire diocese was measured and many congregations had experienced deep losses in membership, I have kept the specific congregations anonymous.

Finally, words of thanks to: the staff and faculty of the Hartford Seminary, especially David Roozen; Bill Anderson and the people of the Episcopal Church Foundation; Bill Newman and the Sociology Department at U. Conn; my parish, Christ Church, Bethany, CT. To my two volunteer editors, Marnie and Kate, blessings. The work is better for their efforts. Of course, all the errors and inadequacies are mine alone.

I dedicate this book to my wife and children, Caron, Kate and Ian, without whose support and love none of this would be possible. And to the late Susan Steinberg, editor of *Faith, Focus and Leadership*, who kept telling me I had a good story to tell, I just needed help in telling it.

CHAPTER ONE

Congregation
growth and decline

In 1963 there were four congregations, all located in the poorer southern part of the diocese to be called New Canterbury. The diocese exists, but it could be almost any in the Church. In 1963, there were strong opinions about the potential of the four congregations among diocesan staff. Two, recently founded in the large town at the center of the region, had the most potential. They would be growing and would get the best support and resources. The neighboring parish, across the small river that ran through the middle of the county, was slated to be closed. It had never really grown, and although it was now almost 100 years old, it was time to stop throwing good money after bad. Finally, there was the parish which served the farming community to the south. It was to be allowed to die of benign neglect. Farming was no longer important to the economy of the region and little potential for growth was seen.

Fast forward 35 years. The two parishes with the "most potential" are preparing to merge after a long struggle to remain independent. The congregation which had been slated to be closed has entered parish status and is one of the strongest congregations in the area. It has become a center of healing ministry, attracting people of many different spiritual perspectives, all of whom are united in feeling supported by this community of faith. The "farming" community has become a place for commuters to the high tech jobs within a one-hour commuting radius and has also grown strong. This parish has a more conservative theological outlook, is centered in "winning souls for Jesus," and is evangelically-oriented while still remaining clearly Episcopal.

What is the difference?

For the first fifteen years there was not a lot. But beginning around 1980, two of the four became committed to a specific path to spiritual growth, a congregational path to holiness. In one case it was a broad-minded approach. Inviting all to come and explore their spiritual lives, it emphasized inclusion, acceptance and diversity. In this congregation there was no one "correct" theological stance. This was distressing to some who needed more clarity. But, to those who constituted the majority of this growing parish, a clear lack of strict norms was just what they needed. They had just one priest during this period.

In the case of the second parish which grew, the congregation committed itself to the renewal movement and to helping individuals develop a personal relationship with Jesus. This emphasis became the focus of congregational life. They emphasized Bible study and small prayer groups and the preaching of the scriptures. Three different priests led them on this journey. Both congregations were clear about their particular call and mission.

The other two have just drifted. The clergy during the period were good, decent leaders. But these communities were unable to develop any particular vision of the best way to go. There was no particular emphasis on building up the spiritual lives of individual members. They weakened while their neighbors grew.

With benefit of hindsight it is easy to see the difference in these parishes. In two communities, the common vision of a path for spiritual growth powered the congregations to become healthy and growing. In the other two this must have been lacking. After all, some would argue, otherwise they would have grown.

This is an old argument. The Episcopal Church is dying, the Episcopal Church has turned the corner; we are about to have a time of unparalleled resurgence, we are about to fall apart in schism, and so on and so forth. I find myself quoting Dickens' A Tale of Two Cities, "It was the best of times and it was the worst of times." This quotation is apt, because it is true. There are ways in which the Episcopal Church is strong at the end of the 20th century and other ways in which it is weak.

The purpose here is to describe a group of congregations which have been very successful in a time when most congregations have been shrinking. The reason is simple to state but complex to describe. I conclude that each of these outstanding congregations has found ways to be holy as a congregation, and in so doing has enabled individual members to deepen their own spiritual lives. Because this process is corporate, I refer to it is as a congregational path to holiness.

There are three such paths for the congregations in this study: one centered in a "Jesus Focused" spirituality, one described by a "Broad-Minded" Christianity, and a third rooted in the special spiritual needs and concerns of a distinct population group.

While these congregations were selected on the basis of numerical growth, investigation found them to be spiritual powerhouses. This runs contrary to a common fallacy in the Episcopal Church that faithfulness leads to decline. As Presiding Bishop Frank Griswold has said, faithfulness leads to growth. And, I believe, where congregations help to deepen the faith lives of individual members, there will be numerical evidence of growth.

This study used objective measures of growth to determine the congregations for in-depth study. In the beginning, I believed I would find seventeen very different stories with no overall pattern. In fact the result revealed not a random group of congregations but rather 17 parishes whose patterns of growth may prove suggestive to many. It is common when studying congregational growth and decline to select samples based on the recommendations of diocesan or national level staff. This is the method I have used in the past. It has the virtue of giving the researcher a very promising sample of congregations. The problem is that they are often the congregations which follow the favored policies of the diocesan staff. The sample is rarely objective. Contrary to our anti-numerical intuitions, this study suggests that numerical measures can be used to identify spiritually strong congregations. As numerical data can be gathered and analyzed far more quickly than "nominations," researchers seeking spiritually strong congregations might use a numerical methodology to identify them. "You will know them by their fruits" is a good guiding principle for this work.

The debate over the exact state of the Episcopal Church

continues largely because one can cite statistics to support both a claim to strength and a claim of weakness. In this we are not alone. The Episcopal Church is one of that cluster of religious bodies once known as "mainline Protestant" but recently renamed the "Protestant Mainstream" by some researchers (Hadaway and Roozen, 1995). These denominations have much in common, including some similar understandings about the role of the church in society, memberships with similar socioeconomic characteristics, a sense of historic religious status and dramatic losses in membership since the late 1960s (Caroll and Roof, 1993). The Episcopal Church alone has lost more than one third of its membership since 1967 (The Episcopal Church Annual, 1995). Yet, within our church some local congregations have grown quite dramatically during this same time period.

Possible explanations for this difference abound. Some argue that the growth of these congregations results from following the principles of the "Church Growth movement" (McGavran and Arn, 1977). One internal Episcopal Church study suggests that increases in numbers are a result of a congregational decision to be "a community which serves others best" (Schwab, Rowthorn and Docker, 1991). Others see local demographic conditions as key, believing that "if there in an increase in the kind of people who usually like the Episcopal Church in an area then you will grow." (Thompson, Carroll and Hoge, 1993) Still others argue that those congregations which grow are those which demand the most from their congregants and so draw the religiously serious (Finke and Stark, 1992). These tend to be the more theologically conservative congregations. Yet, in reality, each perspective only explains the growth of some of the congregations studied. Some conservative Episcopal congregations have shrunk. Some parishes in high growth suburbs are not thriving. Some liberal communities of faith have grown dramatically. Each of the potential explanations for growth and decline serves to explain only a portion of the whole. Clearly, a more comprehensive understanding of the situation is needed.

Hadaway and Roozen (1995) argue that "oldline" Protestant congregations which are growing require a more complex understanding. They assert that these churches fall into one of four categories: congregations that mimic "market-driven" evangelical churches; congregations that are in highly positive demographic situations; congregations that serve "special purpose" niche groups; and those that are "spiritually oriented" but theologically liberal (pp.80-81). This study attempts to test if this hypothesis is correct. In one diocese of the Episcopal Church I examined the 17 congregations forming the top 10% in terms of growth in baptized membership, growth in the number of households, growth in worship attendance, and increase in budget from 1963-1993. I sought to understand why these congregations had grown dramatically during a time period in which 80% of the congregations in that diocese suffered losses in membership.

As will be seen, these congregations did fall into three groups similar to those proposed by Hadaway and Roozen. Seven are deeply spiritually oriented within a more classically liberal framework. Five are similar to the growing evangelical congregations of the conservative Protestant ethos. One of the congregations, the only urban case, serves an ethnic community, a "special purpose" niche, while another fits the "special purpose" case in serving a largely elderly community. The remaining three parishes are probably statistical anomalies resulting from being the three smallest congregations in the sample. In addition, it is critical to remember that the growth of most of these congregations has been aided by a high degree of skill on the part of local leadership. In all, clergy and lay leaders encouraged their congregations to adapt to changing conditions when making decisions about the nature of local congregational programming. In particular they focused on the increased desire among individuals for spiritual growth, a phenomenon evident since about the mid-1980s.

CHAPTER TWO

Background: why some churches grow when others do not

For years there has been a debate about the exact sources of congregational growth and decline among the scholars whose life work it is to understand local churches. While much of this discussion has taken place within the academy it has had a profound effect on national and diocesan mission strategy. These are the men and women who write the books, lead the workshops, and publish the articles which are read by bishops, national church staff and Canons for Mission. It is a complex debate because the congregations themselves are complex. Yet it is critical background for anyone trying to develop congregational growth strategy because these thinkers have framed the discussion.

It is important to begin with definitions. McKinney and Hoge (1983) summarize the debate regarding the traditional sociological approach to congregational studies this way: "The most influential conceptualization of the problem has involved distinguishing 'contextual' from 'institutional' factors and cross-cutting them with the distinction of 'local' versus 'national' to form four sets of factors— national contextual, national institutional, local contextual and local institutional. The research has usually aimed at identifying the strongest determinants within each of the four categories and estimating the relative strength of the four" (p.51).

This is important because many diocesan mission development strategies are based on some or all of these perspectives.

Institutional factors are those under the control of the organization itself. These forces, imposed at either the national or local level, can include the use of mandated books of worship across a denomination, ordination policies, treatment of gay and lesbian persons, stances toward scripture, church school curriculum, evangelism and posture towards newcomers. They may be national or local.

Contextual factors are outside the control of the denomination or congregation, and may include growth or decline in the population of a local area, change in the age, income and ethnic composition of a community, or changes in general social attitudes nationally over time, in such areas as the desirability of attending worship, or of being a "moral" person. Those sociologists favoring national factors assume that the growth or decline of local congregations is primarily a result of major trends on the regional or national level. Those favoring local trends see the growth or decline of congregations as independent of national or regional factors.

Contextual Schools of Thought

The earliest representative of the "national contextual school" was Alexis de Tocqueville (1840), familiar to many, recognized both the dynamism and intensity of the American religious environment. Herberg's *Protestant, Catholic, Jew* (1960) saw the United States as uniquely religious and predicted it would continue to be so, with these three traditions continuing to describe the American religious experience. Iannaccone (1991) noted the U.S. has one of the highest religious participation rates in the world. In his model, all religious organizations should continue to grow equally as the overall religiosity of the society creates a "rising tide" which would lift all boats. This would happen as population increased irrespective of institutional differences. Of course, the solution to the problem of congregational growth is not this simple.

Within the national contextual group others see an increasing melding of religious traditions leading to an emergent civil religion. This group predicts the death of local congregations and their replacement with a vague morality without organization. Alstrom (1972), Parsons (cited in Warner, 1993) and Berger (1969) argue variations on this theme. Still others argue a "secularization with modernization" approach to the theory of national religious development. In simpler language, this means that as we become more affluent, churches will shrink because we will have less "need" for God. This view argues we will become too educated for this "myth of God" to continue to influence us. This is based on one interpretation of the European experience in which low levels of church attendance seem to correlate with modernization (Iannaccone, 1991). Bellah *et al.* (1985) see this as an outcome of increasing individualism.

Roof and McKinney's *American Mainline Religion: Its Changing Shape and Future* (1987) argues this case. They see American religious history as divided into two periods, before and after the "religious turning point of the 1960s" (p.4). According to them, the major churches in America were those which, beginning with the colonial era, represented the cultural mainstream. They had large numbers and were roughly divided (following Herberg) into Protestants, Catholics and Jews, with the first two most important and the latter influential beyond its numbers. The conventional view is that each of these groups grew more influential from the colonial era until the 1960s when, due to a radical culture shift, they began losing numbers and perhaps their claim to be the mainline (pp.11-13). Roof and McKinney (1987) conclude that from the 1960s on religion became, and will become, a less influential factor in American life as the culture becomes more secular; and that local congregations will shrink. That has not proven to be the case.

This recognition has led others to argue that the national context describes an increasing support of religious belief and membership. Greeley (1989) and the Gallup organization (cited in Hadaway and Roozen (1995) cite data to argue that very high levels of religious activity in America continues. There is also an increase in the strength of "conservative" churches (Finke and Stark, 1992; Halvorson and Newman, 1994; Kelly, 1972).

Others favor classic demographic explanations for denominational growth and decline: "As your population grows so shall your church." Newman and Halvorson (1991) note that the concentrations and relative strengths of denominations have been fairly constant over time and that growth and decline is largely due to regional population changes. Roozen (1979) argues that the age composition of a community or region is determinative.

All of the national contextual approaches predict that the relative ranking of American religious bodies will remain as it has been for the past 200 years, allowing for regional variations related to population growth differences in areas of denominational strength.

In understanding denominational culture there is a distinction between those who favor "national contextual" versus "national institutional" explanations of congregational growth and decline. Those favoring national contextual factors, beyond the control of the denomination, see the denominations as relatively static and passive bodies that are acted upon by changes, whether cultural or demographic. Those favoring national institutional factors see denominations as changing better to thrive within a changing context. In other words, denominations must change or die.

This understanding would be supported by Finke and Stark (1992) who argue that the best explanation of denominational growth and decline is to be found in the willingness of denominations to adapt to "religious markets." Those bodies that adapt well will grow, and those that do not will shrink. They further argue that the higher the perceived religious benefit—the classic example being assurance of eternal life—the greater the number of religious adherents. Chaves and Cann (1992) and Warner (1993) also have written articles supporting the view that denominations should be viewed as functioning within a religious market. This bothers many people who believe that one's denominational behavior should be based on "truth," but it has a lot to commend it, even if only as a thinking tool.

Some argue that the simple decision to plant new

churches leads to growth. This thinking led the Episcopal Church to adopt the Decade of Evangelism. Marler and Hadaway (1993) argue that denominations choosing to plant new congregations will grow. They contrast the growth of the membership in the Assemblies of God and Southern Baptist Convention with the decline in membership of the Methodist and Presbyterian Churches as an example of national institutional policy affecting church growth. Greer (1993) suggests the lack of an evangelism strategy may help explain the decline in Methodist and other mainline denominational bodies.

Institutional Schools of Thought

Local institutional factors are those under the control of the local congregation. One example is the age structure of the congregation. Are the people mostly elderly? Are they younger families with children? Is there a mix? Does the congregation reflect the neighborhood? These differences are often determined by congregational programs such as church school, adult education classes, or parish based home care and nursing. Other local institutional factors include the effectiveness of the priest, whether the congregation sets goals for evangelism, and various program emphases (McGavran and Hunter, (1980); McGavran and Arn, 1977). An early summary of the effect of local institutional factors is Hoge and Roozen's Understanding Church Growth and Decline (1979). Two less formal studies on Episcopal Churches also have taken the view that it is these choices, priest and programming, which are most important (Schwab, Rowthorn and Docker, 1991; Stebinger, 1990). Hadaway (1993) argues that evangelistic programming is the single most important predictor of congregational growth, but that it cannot stand alone. Donahue and Benson (1993) cite program quality, especially in education, as well as congregational climate as the key factors based on the study Effective Christian Education (Benson and Elkin, 1990).

Local contextual factors, especially population changes, are not under the control of the local congregation or the denomination. While these largely are parallel to classic demographic categories, they also include aggregate denominational growth and decline. Hoge and Roozen, (1979, ch. 9, 10, 11) see local contextual factors as determinative. McKinney and Hoge (1983) find that much of the difference in congregational growth or decline in one United Church of Christ sample was due to "contextual" factors beyond the control of the local congregation. These include: size of community, years since founding of congregation, change in median household income within the community, ethnicity, the percentage of school-age children, and changes in the demographic composition of the local area. Hadaway (1991) supports this view, even while examining less important local institutional factors relating to growth.

Conclusion

The debate is complex. The best balance may be found in Marler and Hadaway's (1993) work on the effects of new congregational development. They argue that denominations that make a concerted effort to grow will do so, while others will be the passive recipients of the winds of demographic change. This seems to be close to the mark. However, neither the "institutional" nor the "contextual" school seems to be able to account for all the evidence.

Hadaway and Roozen seek to resolve this dilemma in *Rerouting the Protestant Mainstream* (1995), by arguing that a mix of factors account for the selective growth of a few of the "oldline" congregations. The congregations within the oldline tradition that do grow will fall into four categories, three of which are market sensitive (pp. 80-81). Market sensitive refers to congregations which intentionally program to meet the spiritual needs of the membership and of those they would like to be members. Most of us use the term evangelism to describe this activity. The non-market sensitive growing congregations are those in demographic settings where growth is easy. For example, these would be in high growth suburban areas with a demographic mix similar to that of the denomination in question. This finding is supported by Thompson (1991), who shows that in a rural or urban area these congregations would not be likely to grow.

Growing oldline congregations will follow one of three paths. The first includes congregations that imitate the market-driven evangelical churches. These congregations tend to be self-consciously conservative in theological outlook, somewhat oppositional with regard to the liberal denominational structure, and clear about the need to offer diverse programming to help individuals become more spiritual. The second group comprises special purpose churches serving small and unique market niches. This group might include Hispanic congregations, or those catering to twenty-somethings in urban settings. The final group consists of spiritually-oriented mainstream congregations. These are unapologetically liberal congregations with a deep commitment to spiritual growth through meaningful worship. The assumption is that there is a market for such congregations in persons of a liberal yet spiritual outlook. Hadaway and Roozen believe that the latter growth strategy should be pursued by the mainstream churches seeking growth in membership. This view fits well with those who would take a market approach to congregational growth strategies.

Hadaway and Roozen argue that the latter three strategies will work because they conform to the perceived ethos of those who might attend mainstream protestant congregations. The market-driven evangelical subset will grow for all the reasons given by Finke and Stark (1991) and others who have studied conservative church growth. However, these will not be dominant in the more traditionally liberal side of the protestant continuum because relatively fewer persons with this religious orientation will be found there. The special purpose congregations will grow because they will seek to work with previously under-served clusters of individuals. The largest group will be the spiritually-oriented ones. These will serve the growing group of spiritual liberals who are seeking more than social justice and dry worship. Hadaway and Roozen imply there is a pent-up demand for this type of religious community which will flow towards any congregation offering such a program (pp. 80-81). The authors suggest that these congregations will grow because the population of the groups which might provide members is growing. This is different from the "liberal establishment" population which has heretofore provided much of the membership of these denominations.

For most of the past 30 years the Episcopal Church acted like a shrinking denomination without a market-related growth strategy. Yet there are congregations within the church that grew. By and large these were the ones which saw a spiritual need and met it. They tended to fall into the three broad categories predicted by Roozen and Hadaway; however, while these sociologists made an excellent informed guess, their hypothesis was too abstract to support the planning needs of actual congregations. The key is in the details. And the details are what this study seeks to discover.

CHAPTER THREE

How to find the answer: the people and parishes that supplied it

Most studies of congregational growth and decline fall into one of two categories. Some projects take all of the numerical data available and run it through various statistical analyses. The advantage of this method is that a large number of congregations can be examined. The drawback is that the researchers rarely talk with the actual church members. Thus conclusions are based largely on number crunching.

Other researchers select a group of congregations, go and study them and then write up the cases and draw conclusions. The good news here is that actual people are the source of the information. The problem is that the congregations are usually selected through a subjective nomination process. In other words, researchers call up people who know, who then suggest wonderful congregations to study.

In this study parts of both methods were combined to gain the objectivity of numerical selection without losing the wealth of information available from talking to people.

Sources of Information

In order to try to understand why some Episcopal congregations grew during a time when most did not, I gathered both measurable facts known as quantitative data which are usually manifested as numbers, and opinions known as qualitative data which are usually obtained through reading and interviews. The numbers came primarily from two sources: the United States Bureau of the Census and the parochial reports submitted by each Episcopal congregation annually. Additional data on the location of Episcopalians was derived from a series of 1963 studies compiled for each congregation as part of a diocesan-wide study of New Canterbury. The information from these three sources was then used to select the congregations to be studied and to evaluate the demographic hypothesis that congregations grow primarily because of growing population. Once the congregations were selected, I gathered additional quantitative data about parish and community. Each congregation was visited, and interviews with key lay leaders were conducted to gather the subjective or qualitative data. All of the information together was used to determine what, if any, characteristics were distinctive about these congregations.

The Annual Parochial Report is the best source of information on congregational budget, membership and worship attendance. Every congregation in the Episcopal

Church is required to submit to its diocese an annual Parochial Report which is then forwarded to the national church. These reports have been stable in format for the entire study period, so comparisons can be made between different years. A great deal of information on the number of members in the local congregation, both as individuals and as households, is reported. Categories include: total baptized membership; total communicants; and total adult communicants in good standing. The number for total baptized members is the most comprehensive membership number. Total adult communicants in good standing counts the number of persons who have made adult reaffirmations of faith and attend worship six times a year or more. This number is often used to count "active" members. Data for total number of households was also collected to test the possibility that change in membership is related to a decreasing average size of household. Each congregation tracks worship attendance through reporting the actual count of the number of persons at worship on four key Sundays: the first Sunday of Advent, the first Sunday of Lent, Easter Day and Pentecost. This number is part of the report. Financial data is also gathered, with extensive reporting of audited budget figures including: income from pledges; income from plate offerings; endowment income; and income from other sources. This is summarized in the figure called net disposable budget income. In this study this number is called "budget." Data on church-school enrollment, the number and types of services, affiliated organizations, the number of baptisms, confirmations, funerals, and weddings are also gathered. These data are summarized in the diocesan journal of New Canterbury each year. Some people, especially clergy, argue the parochial report is more a matter of wishful thinking than accurate data keeping. This may be true, but since this study was based on comparisons over time, I have assumed the "fudge factor" was applied in a consistent fashion over time.

The Congregational Selection Process

For this study, more than 160 congregations in the New Canterbury diocese were evaluated. This diocese was selected because it had been extensively studied in the early 1960s, which increased dramatically the amount of potentially useful information. Data on total baptized members, total number of households, worship attendance, and budget were collected from the diocesan journals for 1963 and 1993.

These years were chosen because the residential location of each Episcopalian in these years was also available, due to the comprehensive diocesan study done of 1963, and the 1993 mailing list for the diocesan newspaper. This might have proved important had it turned out that church growth was directly related to town growth in New Canterbury. This turned out not to be the case.

I needed some number to use to sort out the congregations which grew most rapidly over the 30 year period under study. To this end I created a number which I called the growthscore. While the following description may seem arcane and peculiar, I believe that it could be easily used to examine other dioceses or groups of congregations with an eye to selecting interesting congregations for study.

To arrive at the growthscore I first computed the percentage change in baptized membership, households, worship attendance and budget. Congregations were sorted in ascending order on each of these variables and given a score based on the percentile of change for that number. The bottom 10% in terms of change in worship attendance were given a one and the top 10% were given a ten, with the other congregations given ranked scores accordingly. This procedure was followed for the four variables: change in worship attendance; change in budget; change in baptized membership; and change in households. These scores were added for each congregation and divided by four to produce the growthscore. Because of some missing data from the Parochial Reports of a few congregations, only 156 congregations could have growthscores computed. Finally, the entire 156 congregations for which this analysis could be done were ranked in ascending order according to the growthscore. The top 10% were then selected for further study. The last congregation included in the study was the top urban congregation in terms of the growthscore. It was included despite the fact that the congregation was just out of the top 10%, because with so many urban congregations in the Episcopal Church, it is important to see what we could learn from the top urban congregation in this diocese.

Having crunched all the numbers, I wanted to hear the stories of each congregation to try to understand why they had grown. My visits to the parishes consisted of a tour of the facility and an interview with a group of lay leaders at each site. In addition, one-half of the Churches in this sample were visited on Sunday morning for worship. It would have been optimal to worship with every congregation. Time constraints made this impossible.

The interviews with lay leader groups were the most important source of information. The numerical analysis had yielded a list of names which might or might not prove interesting. Now the stories of these high-growth congregations needed to be gathered. To this end a group of laity was selected by the clergy in charge of each selected congregation. The hope was that by getting answers to a series of directed questions the causes of congregational growth could be discovered.

The clergy were contacted and asked to gather a group of no fewer than four and no more than ten lay leaders. They were asked to include some persons who had been members for the entire 30-year study period. This group would provide a history of the congregation over the past 30 years. The interviews were conducted utilizing a questionnaire. Areas covered included:

a participant description
a general history of the congregation over the
    past 30 years
the nature of the congregation in the mid-1960s
the nature of the congregation at present
changes in congregational composition
changes in the community
strengths
weaknesses
conflict management styles
clergy leadership
other leadership
times of vitality and special problems
worship
preaching
stewardship
pastoral care
evangelism
education
outreach.

A final question asked for any important information which may not have been included in the questionnaire. The complete set of guidelines is contained in Appendix 1. The interviews lasted between 90 minutes and two hours each.

The participant groups consisted of senior lay leaders, many of whom had been in the congregation between 15 and 30 years, with some lifelong members being in their eighties. Quite often newer members also participated. These persons had all been involved heavily in the life of the congregation and generally were excellent oral historians. Notes from the interviews were recorded and other supporting materials were collected if offered.

Congregational Descriptions

The basic descriptions of the congregations and the communities in which they are located show these congregations could have been located anywhere. The sketch of each parish includes a description of the physical plant, changes in the size of the congregation over time, and brief demographic and social descriptions of the communities in which each congregation is located, including such items as average household income, minority percentage of the population, and percentage of college graduates. In addition, I have included the descriptions of the people who were interviewed for each congregational study. The descriptions are found in Appendix 4.

For purposes of comparison it might be helpful to look at the Diocese of New Canterbury as a whole. The average or mean diocesan annual parish budget in 1963 was $30,000 ($139,000 in 1993 dollars). The median budget in the diocese, exactly halfway between the biggest and smallest, as measured by size of budget, in 1963 was $21,000 ($92,000 in 1993 dollars). In 1993 the average budget was $166,000 and the median budget $123,000. The average baptized membership was 768 in 1963 and 457 in 1993. The median membership was 505 in 1963 and 348 in 1993. The average worship attendance in 1963 was 260 and 194 in 1993. The median worship attendance was 210 in 1963 and 157 in 1993.

New Canterbury as a state was 7.2% African-American in 1990. The median household income was $38,269. A remarkable 20.6% of the population had graduated from college statewide in 1990.

CHAPTER FOUR

The first path: spiritually broad-minded congregations

The group interviews revealed that most of the congregations in the study had behaved in one of three ways. Most had followed a spiritually broad-minded path that emphasized diversity and inclusion. The second largest group utilized a Jesus focused spirituality to empower the congregations. Finally, two congregations had chosen to organize their programs around the needs of a special purpose group. Hadaway and Roozen (1995) suggest, in part, that specific congregational program choices will lead to growth. These sociologists were vague as to what these choices might be, not being sure what exact programs would lead to growth. However, lay leaders interviewed could often cite specific plans and policies which led to positive change.

Because these varied from congregation to congregation I have let each parish tell its own story. Usually the case begins with some description of the historical highlights of the past 30 years and then moves to the present. Sometimes the order is different to reflect the emphases of those who were interviewed.

This first and largest group, seven of the 17, had chosen a path I label "spiritually broad-minded." This path emphasized individual spiritual growth within a deeply congregational context. They were characterized by a broad-minded openness to a diversity of spiritual paths. While most were willing to accept people who supported any path of a positive spiritual nature, the clergy and lay leadership were quite orthodox Christians in their core values. Despite the criticisms of some of their more evangelical neighbors, all of these congregations were populated with Eucharistically-centered Anglicans who believe in the basic tenets of the Christian faith.

These seven congregations share a number of attributes as revealed by the interviews. Their broad-minded spirituality was accepting of persons with widely-varying theological and religious beliefs. This openness was not only accepted, it was celebrated. Diversity was a word which was often used with approval during the interview conversations. Theologically, for them, the Holy Spirit was most important. This more flexible aspect of the deity, less well-defined than Jesus, fit the predispositions of these congregations best. They were far more comfortable with calling the second person of the Trinity Christ, rather than Jesus, reflecting a more ethereal spirituality. These congregations tended to have fairly active social outreach ministries serving the poor and needy. All of the congregations described the preaching of the clergy as excellent. Finally, skilled leadership, lay and ordained, was present in all of these congregations.

Now to the stories.

Resurrection, Haven

In the mid-1960s, the congregation was already middle-sized, with a worship attendance of about 150 on a typical Sunday. Plagued with a chronic parking problem due to highway renovation at the site of the old church in Unionville, the congregation built their new building in some vacant fields in the town next door, Haven. The move was difficult, because at the time the number of members was stable or even declining slightly. The budget was $14,000 ($64,800 in 1993 dollars) per year and, although the membership rolls showed over 500 members, less than one-third were present on an average Sunday. In 1972, a new, very pastoral, family-oriented priest came to the congregation. He was an excellent preacher but a poor administrator. Members began to become more active in running the congregation. People began to initiate new projects, even though there was "no plan." The focus was on social as well as religious life, with the congregation at the center of lots of picnics, progressive dinners and fairs.

This rector left in 1983. The search committee for the next rector sought someone who was "more spiritual" than his predecessor. They looked for someone who would strengthen outreach, Christian education and adult spiritual development. J. W., the current rector, has done all of this. Described as "extremely spiritual with a kind of Quaker quietude," he has brought a far greater spiritual seriousness to the congregation than was there previously. He is a good communicator who helps people feel the presence of the Holy Spirit. His great gift is in spiritual formation although not with any particular theological bias. He gives space to people and helps them arrive at their own conclusions. His sermons are personal and emphasize the human experience. The congregation now has three worship services, two on Sunday and one on Saturday. Each is "quite different spiritually," yet each is integral to the overall ministry of the congregation.

J. W. has helped to establish a strong music ministry. This has become increasingly important to the congregation. There is also a far greater outreach ministry, which has included sponsoring a Laotian refugee family and links to the Lakota Sioux. There is a newly funded director of religious education, and the congregation is positive about the present situation. While the congregation knows that money is a perpetual problem, it is not causing the conflict it did in the past, because of a confidence that "God will provide what we need."

It is worth noting that the congregation is now over 300 on a typical Sunday and the annual budget is $219,000. Most of the increase has come since the arrival of the latest rector, and each year more and more people come to worship on an average Sunday, even though this congregation has no formal evangelism program. This happens, the interviewees assert, because it is a congregation where "we are helping newcomers to get spiritually formed."

Resurrection, Haven has the combination of liberality and spiritual intensity suggested by the "Broad-Minded" typology. Worship is perceived to be of high quality with excellent music and preaching and a diversity of formats. Individuals are given space to grow as they need. The congregation is led by a rector who is good at communicating spiritual strength without being too insistent. This has drawn in many new people, and the congregation has grown dramatically in the past 12 years while engaging in no formal program of evangelism.

St. John's Church, Oldtown

St. John's Church, Oldtown, moved its building in 1965. At that time the worship attendance was about 110 on a typical Sunday and the budget was $16,000 ($74,000 in 1993 dollars) per year. The membership was listed as being about 425. Although the diocese wanted the congregation to merge with the church in Haven, they refused and raised the funding to move and renovate their buildings. Money was tight, and for a time, the congregation shared a clergyperson with Haven. A new rector came in 1971, after the move had been accomplished. There was conflict during this cleric's tenure and the congregation did not grow particularly, although it did not shrink. In 1978 the present rector came, and a period of growth began which continues to this day. The budget increased to $138,000 and the worship attendance has almost doubled, to over 200 on a typical Sunday.

The congregation is described by the interview group as "a place that you want to come." It has a large percentage of children, 30% of the main worship service congregation, and the people as a whole are described as "younger, vibrant, and energized" compared to 30 years ago. The arts are important. A diversity of music, including jazz, has been incorporated into the parish's worship life. The congregation has also sponsored art shows, dramatic presentations, and poetry readings. However, the interview group asserted that underlying the congregation's success is a wide array of educational offerings, including Education for Mission and Ministry (EFM), a four year course in Christianity; retreats; and spirituality groups of all types.

The rector is perceived as an important factor in the growth of this thriving congregation. He is described as a superb preacher who is most opinionated. "You need some wits to follow his sermons," was one positive comment. He is seen as very moved by the Holy Spirit and is "uplifting" to those in need or crisis. He can be liberal and comical, but it is clear that he approaches worship and prayer with a great deal of seriousness. A priority is for everyone to be a part of worship. To this end, one person noted, they have had American flags at appropriate services, even though that is not the preference of the rector. There are many acolytes, and an effort is made to include children in worship. Healing is also a part of the life of this congregation, again led by the rector. St. John's is a place where people care about each other, and will encourage other members to be more serious about their life in faith

Oldtown believes in outreach, with ministries to battered women, a food bank, and a counseling center. However, there is a sense that more could be done; it is a parish with "high standards for everything, whatever we do, we do well." Everyone is encouraged to be involved in addition to attendance at worship.

Interestingly, there is no formal evangelism program, nor is any special attention paid to the stewardship of money. The congregation clearly believes that if the programs are diverse, and people are encouraged to give, the congregation will grow, and people will give enough to support the ministry and program.

St. John's is an enthusiastic, diverse, growing congregation. While there are no overtly stated standards for behavior, a commitment to living a deeper and more serious Christian life is assumed by the rector and people. This atmosphere has proved to be attractive to many, as the congregation has grown dramatically while not actively seeking growth. St. John's certainly emphasizes individual spiritual growth in a liberal context of broad-minded spirituality.

Resurrection, Portsmouth

The most significant event for this congregation in the 1960s was the closing of the neighboring parish of St. John's and its reintegration into Resurrection. St. John's, South Hampton was founded by Resurrection in the 19th century. The hard feelings about the "forced" merger took over five years to heal. The perception was that Portsmouth was "very expensive," while the Resurrection people were seen by some as "country bumpkins." The two communities had "little in common." For a long time after the "merger," during the 1960's, the congregation was "very stiff and staid" with only ten or 12 people at Sunday worship. Mostly from one family, these active parishioners carried out most of the tasks of the congregation. Conflict with these lay leaders often resulted in the departure of individuals or families. Contributing to the instability was the experience of having had five different clergy in charge over the period under study. Two were described as "nice but lacking in charisma." One was good and one, the predecessor to the current rector, was described as "a troubled person who had a difficult time relating to people."

The congregation has changed significantly since 1985, when the current rector arrived. There has been tremendous growth, especially among younger families. The congregation had become "friendly and intimate," with a more casual style than had been the case in the past. The people are described as flexible and like a family. Conflicts still occur but feel "more like disagreements, they don't fester." More people are involved, with a wide distribution of roles and responsibilities among the entire congregation.

At the core of this new vitality is a spirituality undergirding the life of the congregation. This spirituality was rooted in a conviction that people are different from one another and have different opinions, but that God calls them to go beyond this to a deeper unity. Pledging, which had been seen as "dues for the club," is now a matter of "faith and individual growth." There are a strong and active EFM group, adult forum, and church school, all emphasizing God's love. The congregation is a place where "questions get answered." A feeling of "warmth and tolerance and helpfulness" in the midst of a serious spirituality describes the overall sense of the congregation.

The role of the current rector is held to be key to this. Her sermons relate the "Bible to everyday life" in a manner so effective some people even take notes. The sermons were seen as "sending us out with a message every week, something you wanted to share with a friend." Worship has become more reverent and inclusive, with lay people involved in many roles, a change from the past. Finally, the rector lives out her sermons in the day-to-day interactions with the people, with members of the congregation, and with the community at large. "Everyone knows her" was one comment. "She is there before you know you need her," was another.

While it is true that the introduction of an enthusiastic, competent cleric after a period of conflict can help a congregation, Resurrection's revitalization was rooted in a deep spirituality as well. Good sermons and pastoral care helped, but the strong sense of the congregation was that the openness and tolerance of that spirituality and the encouragement of questions were also key.

Resurrection is a congregation in which the key to growth was having a broad based spirituality which welcomes questions. Liturgy is good; preaching, outstanding; and the rector creates a space into which anyone can come.

St. John's, Lewes

In the early 1960s, St. John's received a large endowment which would have a great impact on its life. Equivalent to over ten million in 1990 dollars, it made the congregation financially secure for the foreseeable future and began a tradition of parish outreach to the needy which has continued to the present time. The congregation was seeking a new rector at the time of my visit but the interviewees saw three distinct periods of parish life during the past 30 years. Each roughly coincided with the tenure of a particular rector. The 1960s focused on social action. The congregation was linked informally to an African-American congregation in a neighboring city to whom they gave significant gifts of both time and money. The rector was involved with the civil rights struggle, traveling to the South to march and organize. The preaching was political. The congregation was smaller and had three services which were combined for a time on the assumption that more people in the nave would be good for the congregation.

During the 1970s the congregation focused on family life and the congregational community. The first full time clerical assistant came at the end of this period. Lewes itself increased greatly in population and in the number of professional people in the town. The congregation at this time "became like a family" and continued to grow in numbers. There were many church picnics and fairs with the three "F's" at the center of life, "fun, food and faith."

The last stage, from 1980 to 1992, was characterized by a deepening spirituality and an expanded educational ministry. Music became a larger part of worship, with both a traditional format and a contemporary music group. Many people went on retreat and especially became involved in EFM and Cursillo, another education and renewal movement. There is "something for everybody." Diversity is a word which came up frequently in reference to outreach, education, church school, and worship. It even affected outreach to the extent that the parish was providing much of the leadership on town committees, and saw this as part of its spiritual role. This sense of broad-based spirituality allowed some to like Bach and others to favor tambourines, and yet stay in the same community. "Spirituality is the foundation of everything else," noted one interviewee.

One key to this was preaching, which was far more biblical than that of the two previous rectors. This biblical focus is linked to everyday life and to telling stories related to real-life experiences. This was seen as different from the bland or civil rights-oriented preaching of the previous two clergy. Yet, this preaching, when linked to the strong teaching ministry, allowed for great variations in the congregation in terms of beliefs and activities. There was much more engagement in the decision-making process, and people were encouraged to do things on their own. In summary, the interviewees felt that a combination of a deep faith commitment, supported by good leadership, preaching, and a strong educational program, linked to a broad-mindedness as to how that faith might be manifested within this part of the Christian tradition, was key to the continued strength and growth of the congregation.

While not quite as explicitly liberal as the previously discussed congregations of the broad-minded, St. John's, Lewes does emphasize diversity in its programming and life. Thus, it is "liberal" in its sensibilities. Certainly, there is no specific doctrinal norm, and individual growth is a priority, placing this parish on the broad-minded path. However, there is a marked conservative leadership element present in this congregation which was lacking in Haven, Oldtown, and Portsmouth.

St. Luke's, Bethlehem

The congregation in the 1960s was mostly elderly blue collar workers with only two preschoolers, a key measure of vitality in most religious communities. The current rector was sent as vicar, clergy who serve at the pleasure of the Bishop, because the congregation needed a financial subsidy from the diocese to pay his salary. In 1965, he came with orders from the diocese to close the congregation. He is still present, and now the congregation is self-supporting with no need for financial help from the denomination.

Over this period the congregation's attitude changed, while serving largely the same constituency. Healing was a word which kept reappearing in the interview. "A lot of unhappy people have gotten happy, been healed," was the comment of one respondent. This was viewed as a systemic, as well as individual, change. Another spoke of the ways in which "we are all sharing in the different tasks." This was related to explaining how, in a congregation in which clerical leadership had dominated, there was now a shared leadership style. In addition, the congregation had attracted younger people with children. "They were always there, but they did not feel welcome." These changes happened gradually over time. Unlike some of the other congregations in this group, there were no distinct phases of congregational history over the past 30 years, probably due to the presence of a single priest in charge for over 20 of these 30 years.

Currently, the congregation is described as diverse, child-friendly, and a place to learn spiritual and moral values. "All of us are wounded and have been healed. We are not all the same but there is an unconditional acceptance of who and where you are." The passing of the peace, a time of greeting within the worship service is "the longest known." This reflects the comfort felt by the members, who see the congregation as "home."

Children are another focus of St. Luke's. "Our kids tell us 'we like it here.'" An excellent church school and nursery school programs were keys to congregational growth. The congregation believes that denying children religious training is denying them free will. Children are incorporated into the worship service as readers and liturgical assistants and many teenagers still are active during a time of life when most move away from familial religious expression.

Yet, the congregation is reported as being closely "focused on God, not just on parish life." "People seriously try to live out their baptismal vows." The Episcopal service of baptism includes six vows which the entire congregation reaffirms at each baptismal service, usually at least four times a year. "We live out our ministry not just on Sunday morning" was another comment, reflecting the desire to move the respondent's faith life beyond just Sunday worship. Sermons are "rooted in scripture and inspired by the Holy Spirit, while still remaining topical and down to earth." Worship is also seen as excellent, with lots of participants and variety.

St. Luke's Bethlehem fits many of the parameters for a high-growth liberal congregation. While the community is very spiritually centered with good worship and excellent preaching, there is a noticeable absence of "Jesus" language in the comments of the interviewees. Values language is used in place of biblical language, and the Holy Spirit is the favored person of the Christian Trinity. Yet, the congregation has grown quite dramatically in an area which is not demographically suited to the typical Episcopalian congregation. This supports the idea that there is a liberally-oriented spiritual pattern which leads to growth. Diversity and individual growth are key. Unlike Oldtown, where a self-conscious religious liberalism is central, here the core experience is healing.

St. Claire's, Ridgewood

The interview group described St. Claire's of 30 years ago as "set in its ways, and having trouble entering the 20th century." The rector had been there over ten years (he would stay 20 more) and there was "entrenchment of the laity." People were having trouble breaking into the leadership circle and the parish was stuck. Words like: "stoic," "hidebound," "rigid," "no place for young people," "God's frozen chosen," and "intimidating" were used. In addition, the town was a small community with little affluence, except for a group of "summer people" who brought income to the largely Italian-American townsfolk.

Then the suburban boom, already apparent closer to the major metropolitan area to the west, hit Ridgewood. The population profile changed, with more management types who were "looser and diverse." "Corporate gypsies" who moved around a lot, they were quicker and more forceful about entering leadership. The population became more affluent and better educated. Yet the parish remained as it was in 1960 until around 1975, when the rector remarried and "rejuvenated." This was the beginning of a period of opening and change, which continues today.

The next rector served from 1980 to 1987. He was "friendlier." While he began a process of change, much of his time was focused on "dealing with a series of personal tragedies among the staff." Still the parish began to open up during the struggle to "try new things."

The present time is described as a "time of outstanding vitality." The parish is currently experiencing all-time highs in worship attendance, an average of 435 at worship on a Sunday, a budget of $541,000 in 1995, and membership at over 1,000 on the rolls for the first time. The congregation cites "diversity" as its key strength. While there is a sense of wealth present, hard to avoid in this very affluent community, the parish is "open to all." In addition, the quality of interpersonal care is quite high. If someone is sick, "people act on the information and visit." A high percentage of the congregation is involved in a program called Stephen Ministries, which trains and deploys lay hospital and home visitors. This has deepened the level of support for anyone in need. Finally, adult education is seen as providing strength to the parish. Education for Ministry, EFM, is active and there are many other adult education offerings.

Much of the current strength is ascribed to the skill of the present rector. Arriving in 1989 from a diocesan staff position, he is seen as an excellent preacher. In addition, he began both Stephen Ministries and EFM in the parish. He manages a staff of nine, who are clearly seen as helping the congregation. While this is to be expected, the current

Rector is "more organized" and a "leader who gets the best out of people." Worship is good, with three clergy preaching in a given month, providing "delightful diversity" according to the interview group.

While the people of St. Claire's, Ridgewood, lacked the theological language of some of the other broad-minded congregations, the emphasis on diversity is a key indicator of the appropriateness of its membership in this group. While the family language and satisfaction with clergy leadership are not unique to this type, it is the inclusion of all people which marks it, especially as the congregation is seen as growing more diverse and inclusive over time. While not as strongly liberal as some of the others, it does fit into this group and meets the criteria of a broad-minded path. It differs from some of the others in this group with its emphasis on program activities. Perhaps this may be a function of its larger size rather than a result of a differing theological emphasis.

St. Matthew's, London

The congregation of St. Matthew's was small in the early 1960s, meeting in a school down the street from the present location of the church complex, and focused on getting a new building constructed. The current location was chosen because "this was a growing part of town." This task was completed, and the next rector, who served from 1967 to 1980, was described as personable and a lot of fun. There was no rectory; there were many social and fundraising activities, and it was viewed as a time when low commitment was acceptable. "You could bring your children to church school and drop them off. You cannot do that anymore." There was some growth, but "he stayed here too long." During this period there were lots of families with children joining the congregation, mirroring the population composition of the neighborhood.

From 1982 to 1990 the parish was served by a rector described as "everybody's friend." He "did everything," a negative trait, but, he also paid off the mortgage and moved the congregation from "aided," needing assistance from the diocese to operate, to independent status. "He could talk about anything," but was described as "over-programmed." The parish had dramatic increases in budget but not in membership during this time period.

The current rector has been in the parish since 1992. His attitude is seen as "down to earth," linked to the everyday. He is "spiritual" and "devoted to religion." These are seen as real positives. He has good people skills, is able to resolve conflict, and is good at getting people to do things. He is not caught up in politics, is very personable, and gets along with "everybody." "The last two years have been a time of huge growth." "We have new families almost every week, and an amazing number of children and babies." There are more people than there have ever been in the history of the congregation.

The current rector's preaching is superb and has many of the characteristics of the spirituality typical of the broad-minded parish. "Something for everyone," was one remark. "Spirituality connected to real life" commented another. "Why I come here" was a common comment about the preaching. Spiritual, yet not "Jesus-centered," this is the broad-minded formula.

As is common in these parishes, St. Matthew's has many outreach programs. On the Sunday of the visit to the congregation, the sanctuary was filled with teddy bears, which were going to the police force in the nearby city to be used to calm victims of child abuse. A large community garden, work with a local children's home, serving at a soup kitchen, and supporting two food banks are also a part of this congregation's outreach program.

Two other characteristics were emphasized. The first is that there was a "kind of synergy" among parish programs. "Nothing is in a box; music people go to outreach and the church school works in the community garden." "No one program stands alone. All seem to feed each other." The other outstanding characteristic is openness to the "theologically disturbed." When pressed for more detail, the interviewees defined this as a willingness on the part of both clergy and people to work with those who are not mainstream in their beliefs. This has helped evangelism because people with any set of beliefs can join.

The rector of St. Matthew's described himself as a conservative Christian "theologically." Yet, the tone of openness to diversity which he sets characterizes this as a broad-minded parish. It has grown largely because of its willingness to work with all people. In addition, the use of the vaguer word "spiritual," as opposed to the more specific "Christian" or "Jesus," to describe the theological orientation of the congregation mark this as a similar congregation to the others in this group. While the rector considers himself "conservative," the congregational leaders see the church as a place where a diversity of individuals can grow without being "pushed."

These broad-minded congregations exhibit many common characteristics. They take spiritual growth very seriously and work very hard to meet the need for individual spiritual growth, a deeply expressed desire of the members. Yet, this growth is diverse in expression. In each of these congregations "diversity" is a word used consistently to describe this broad-minded approach to spiritual issues. This is expressed in a wide range of programming within the congregation, and especially in sermons which approach spiritual and religious issues from a variety of viewpoints. Social outreach is important to each of these congregations, and all seek to serve the poor in tangible ways. Worship is strong. Finally, clerical leadership is strong in meeting the perceived needs of these communities. There is a strong sense on the part of the lay leaders interviewed that without skilled clergy leadership these congregations would not have grown.

While it is true that each of these parishes place a great emphasis on individual spiritual growth in a liberal context, this single choice seems to be only part of the answer. Other factors have contributed to the growth in these congregations. These include preaching and clergy leadership.

CHAPTER FIVE

The second path:
Jesus-focused congregations

The second largest group of congregations, five, have been labeled Jesus-focused. The religious life of these congregations includes four common characteristics. While the broad-minded congregations often use Christ and the Holy Spirit as the central words of their spiritual vocabulary, for these congregations the preferred label for their spiritual focus is Jesus. While Jesus is certainly one of the labels for the second person of the Christian Trinity for all congregations, the person and message of the one who walked in Palestine almost 2,000 years ago is the dominant theme for Jesus-focused congregations.

This leads to a marked seriousness about the authority of the Holy Scriptures of the New Testament, the second characteristic of congregations following this path to holiness. While the broad-minded churches might be fairly liberal in interpreting scripture, seeing it as culture-bound and needing contemporary interpretation, the Jesus-focused congregations see it as having clear authority with very little correction needed. This is congruent with a serious concentration on Bible study as the dominant mode of both children's and adult education. While the broad-minded congregations might present a smorgasbord of offerings, Bible study is the mainstay of the Jesus-focused, with the focus on the historical Jesus who is revealed through scripture. Third, a focus on spreading the "good news of Jesus Christ" marked these congregations as more classically evangelical than the broad-minded. The importance of winning new souls to an orthodox faith in Jesus Christ as Savior was a clear sub-theme, and so too are increased numbers. Finally, in common with the broad-minded group, preaching is perceived as excellent in all of the Jesus-focused congregations. While the expositions of scripture were more centered on Jesus than those of the broad-minded parishes, the sermons were still well grounded in the issues of modern life, as well as clear and well communicated. Some people would describe the sermons as theologically conservative; the preachers would describe these offerings as faithful.

As with the first section, each of the Jesus-focused congregations is presented as a separate case study. The interview results are detailed, beginning with history and then moving to the present. Finally, some summary comments are offered.

St. John's, Constance

In the early 1960s, the congregation of St. John's Church, Constance, was described as "six elderly people and two families." It was "just the old guard." The giving was small, and the budget was low. People were very traditional Episcopalians. Children, who were members of the congregation, grew up and left. "It was all people from town," and things were going along in the usual manner of decline which often leads to consolidation with another congregation after long years of contraction.

In 1968 a new rector came. This person was described as very "charismatic," in this usage an almost technical term, meaning one who "speaks in tongues" and claims a very evangelical and theologically conservative spirituality. While the parish grew, the congregation described the time as "turbulent." "There was a division between those who were charismatic and those who liked church bazaars." In other words, there was a split between those who felt that the center of parish life should be "spiritual," and those who felt that practical issues, such as raising money for the parish budget, should take precedence, the "workers" and the "pray-ers." The congregation was factionalized. Those on the edges left.

This period ended in 1980 with the arrival of the present rector. The turning point, reported by several members of the interview committee, was when "the calling committee decided to dedicate itself to Jesus Christ as its Lord and Savior and the head of the church." This decision, as reported by those who were interviewed, played a large part in the decision to call the present rector. The earlier period had been characterized by significant spiritual growth, but that growth did involve some conflict in the congregation. The new rector had been a member of the congregation and was also dedicated to Jesus Christ as Lord and Savior but was much more conciliatory. The congregation is currently described as "faithful, joyful, healed, and powerful." It is seen as a peaceful, family place, accepting and converting persons, a place where "the Lord lives here in the people, in the building." This congregation is Jesus-focused in a way that is quite profound.

The Jesus-focus of the congregation is evident in the reasons interviewees gave for joining St. John's. "It's a simple place. People can live the Bible here." "We've been healed. Therefore we can reach out to others." "I was a witness to the conversion of the parish 16 years ago." These kinds of comments, which involve a lively sense of the presence of Jesus Christ as Lord and Savior, were common for the interview committee.

The preaching and liturgy are seen as consistent and excellent. The preaching was described as "unforgettable." "'Jesus as Lord' is proclaimed." The sermons were described as not polished, having a single purpose, that purpose being an expression of the Gospel. "They are direct. They are comfortable. They are Biblical. They are not issue-oriented." This is contrasted with the sermons of the previous rector, who is described as "someone who preached carefully created and entertaining sermons, but God was not particularly present." The worship itself is seen as consistent, well done, and impeccable, "meticulous, yet reverent." The music ministry is described as "awesome." Pastoral care is seen as another core. "All our people minister." "There are healing services, afghans for the Dempsey Center. All our people are pastors."

Evangelism is seen as being at the core of this congregation's life. "We are 'one-tool people' who center lives on Jesus Christ, and it overflows into the community." This has created steady growth in the congregation. But the numerical increase is just a sign of deeper growth. The congregation is also involved in the community. The parish house is open. AA meetings are welcomed. Troubled kids are counseled. There is activity seven days a week. The church doors are never locked.

The strengths of the congregation are seen as "people practicing their Christian faith every day." The congregation uses a unanimity rule, in which no decision is made unless all the leadership is unanimous. This is believed to be an expression of the Lordship of Jesus Christ. It is interesting that when asked to describe the congregation, one member of the interview group said, "We are not a family, but a functioning Christian community. This is different from what most people say about their churches." Others felt that the family metaphor was a good one for this congregation. "We are a community of mature Christians." While the word "diversity" was used during the interview, it was a diversity of views within a fairly narrow perspective, around Christian evangelicalism. This is expressed through classic formularies, such as describing the congregation as having a rector "who is part of the body, but Jesus Christ is the Head." When asked to describe the congregation's change over the last 30 years, one person said that "the congregation changed from being a small group to a dynamic community whose focus is on the Lord."

St. John's Church in Constance is a lively, dynamic community thriving in an area of the state which has undergone much economic depression over the past several decades. It is a classic Jesus-focused congregation, in that the word "Jesus" is used over and over again, and seeking Jesus Christ as Lord and personal Savior is the focus of this congregation's life. This pattern of focusing on Jesus has helped this particular community to grow and thrive in a setting in which many other congregations have not.

More conservative theologically than the denomination as a whole, and committed to evangelism, it fits the Jesus-focused mold.

Christ Church, Riverton

When asked what had happened in this congregation over the past 30 years, the response was "we have become a net exporter of people turned on for Jesus Christ." In the early 1960s, Christ Church was viewed as a small congregation of friendly people, and met in a local school. It was begun by a group of families who had left the other large Episcopal church within the town. This group of people felt that there was a need for a more Biblical approach to Scripture. The founding rector began Bible studies and created a "hunger for Scriptural teaching." This ministry continued until 1971.

From 1972 until December of 1989 the second of the three rectors in this time period led the parish. This was the Rev. E. F., an unusually good teacher. "Whenever E. spoke, we had packed houses." This is when the congregation became a regional church going from worshipping in a school, to building a church, to using the local high school auditorium for the main Sunday worship service. This was not by choice. The congregation tried five times to expand its site, but was opposed by the planning and zoning commission. In the mid-1970s the parish began clergy conferences to train other leaders in its method of "serving the Lord." Visitors came from all over the nation and Europe to learn what this congregation had done and to "find examples of what church could be." The rector would not allow lay leaders to come without their clergy. All this was centered in "the Holy Spirit which brings renewal."

The interview group expressed a belief that this rector was absolutely key in this situation. The parish developed a "unanimity principle," in which every person on the Vestry had to agree, or no decision would be made. We were "seeking (to be) a New Testament church." From its inception the congregation viewed itself as atypical. As it grew, the congregation hired two associates who did pastoral care, administration and preaching. The Rev. F. was spending more and more time on the road doing vestry retreats for other churches. As more and more time was spent off-site by Father F., the attendance of the congregation, which had hit a high of around 3,000 per week, started to drop. Finally, he resigned to pursue a full-time independent teaching ministry.

There followed a long interim period of several years, at the end of which the current rector was called. He is also Biblically-centered, and considered to be a person of incredible personal integrity. The key difference between him and Father F. is his desire to remain in the congregation and to focus most of his efforts on current members. The congregation has changed: it is younger; has more families with small children; there is a larger regular Sunday congregation, and the teaching ministry to children is improving. The congregation is making church school for children a priority after many years of focusing on adults. After a period of some turmoil, the congregation is stabilizing. Worship attendance is still around 800 for Sunday morning, no mean feat for a congregation which started with only 50.

Over and over the congregational interviewees stated that the "Word of Jesus is key here." Bible teaching, energy, and the Gospel of Jesus Christ are at the core of their ministry. Jesus Christ, mentioned more often than the

Father or the Holy Spirit, is the key—"His Lordship." We are "committed to the Gospel, to a serious walk with Jesus Christ." Christ Church "focuses on a personal relationship to Christ in which Scripture is central, along with prayer and worship." The role of the clergy is to strengthen the congregation through preaching, keeping the New Testament concept in front of the laity, keeping the church and the faith in the forefront of everyone's consciousness. Ninety percent of the people are involved in evangelism. This is seen as a key aspect of the growth of the congregation.

While Father F. was certainly central to the incredibly expansive growth of the congregation, non-ordained leadership was also crucial. Father F. said that "the goal of the clergy is to equip the lay people." There is a great deal of non-clergy leadership. "If you want it, you start it," was the theme of his ministry. This has caused a lot of different ministries to begin, many successful, some not. All of them, according to the interview group, empowered the people who led them.

It is hard to overestimate the central role of the Rev. F. in the incredible growth of Christ Church in Riverton. A charismatic leader of immense gifts, he drew in people, literally by the bus load, to hear him speak and teach; however, since his departure, the congregation, while shrinking some, has become much stronger in its core group, and is still of considerable size. This is a classic Jesus-focused congregation in that Jesus Christ is the center of everything the congregation does. The Bible is cited on a frequent basis, and there is an evangelical edge to all that they do. Outreach is seen primarily in terms of evangelism, in winning new souls for Christ. Education and pastoral care are also seen in this light. While not every congregation will have as gifted a leader as the Rev. F., once that growth has been created, it can be continued through Jesus-centered and Jesus-focused preaching, teaching and congregational life.

Christ Church, Johnson

In the early to mid-1960s, Christ Church in Johnson was not particularly known for its spiritual life, but rather for its social fellowship. It was described as "not too spiritual." There were three worship services each Sunday. People carted chairs from place to place because the congregation had a larger number of people than its nave could handle. This continued into the mid-1970s.

In 1974, a new rector was needed, and the calling committee decided to highlight spiritual process. They wanted to get involved in "spiritual renewal and growth," and they called a new rector who promoted that aspect of the Christian life. There was a congregational weekend program focusing on renewal known as "Faith Alive," and shortly after it was held, the congregation was described as being completely full. These people were a transient community, and after a period of strong initial growth, worship attendance declined. There were fewer young families, the church school had dwindled, and the congregation was moving down from the high water-mark that it had reached about 1980. Christ Church continued with the same rector until 1987. During the mid-1980s, the congregation as a whole started to be in conflict and decline. There was some bitterness, and the rector at the time was seen as unapproachable and academic. This was stated by the interview group as being a perception, not a truth, but it was a perception that was widespread in that it had caused some problems.

In 1988 the congregation called a new rector. While Father T. as he is called, is a spiritual person, he is seen as being very outgoing, a real people-person, and very much a youth worker. He is perceived as someone who visits new people at home, and puts out a real effort to get involved with them, a major change from his predecessor. "Father T. makes you want to come back," was the comment of one of the members of the interview committee. "The congregation is more open than in the past," said another. "If people can't relate to the rector, they won't come to church. That's why I'm back," said another member of the interview committee. Father T.'s friendliness and ability to relate to people is seen as an important factor in the growth of the congregation. "People enjoy coming back. It's a nice place and they want to be here. Another important factor, is that Father T. never looks down on people, and you never get to the negative."

While certainly the current rector is seen as a factor in the growth of the congregation, it is not just his friendly personality which was described as determinative. The strengths of the congregation included friendliness, knowing people and welcoming kids, not just by the rector but by others. They also included the fact that people's opinions count, that the leadership is much more democratic than in the past. People don't feel lost. Members come up and talk to new people. All of this reflects an intentional emphasis. It is a friendly place. And, unusual for many suburban congregations, single people are made to feel welcome.

There are many spiritual dimensions to the strength of the congregation. The congregation itself is focused strongly on Bible teaching, which is seen as being of very high caliber, on lifting up the light of the Holy Spirit. The congregation is considered to be lively on a day-to-day basis. There is a very strong emphasis on education. The congregation has also proved to be unusually innovative. During the time when I was visiting the congregation, they had made a decision to shift their Lenten study to Friday night, which is an unusual time to do adult and children's education. But it was the perception of the education committee that since most people use Friday night as a time to go out as a family to eat pizza, maybe they would be willing to devote an hour to studying the Holy Scripture and to increasing the faith lives of their children. This was the only congregation in which this researcher had ever heard such a proposal made, and the congregation as a whole was looking forward to it.

The worship in the congregation is termed "completely awesome." In the early 1980s, under the previous rector, worship was seen as being more Pentecostal, involving speaking in tongues and at times livelier, with more alternative music. But the present worship is also seen as very Holy Spirit-centered. The preaching is centered in the Bible, and is described as "bringing things into the '90s," "lively, day to day." "The current rector communicates much better than his predecessor." "He is much more personal." "He brings it to your level, and makes the Bible connected to you. He makes one point and sticks to it." Making the Bible understandable on a day-to-day basis is very important to this congregation. In worship, Jesus is very much the center of the congregational life, and the mood is very up-beat and evangelical.

The congregation presently worships in a space known as "the chapel," across the street from the 200 year old first building. This new chapel was constructed because it was seen as a problem for the children to cross the very busy road that ran between the parish hall and the church itself. It is called "the chapel" because for the congregation the main worship space is the original building, across the street. But in reality it is in the chapel that the community gathers. The decision to do this caused some conflict, but Father T. handled it very diplomatically and very few people left. They had talked about moving the nave across the street, but this proved to be difficult. Money was given, and the chapel was built. The whole decision was handled very democratically, and the congregation emerged from the crisis much stronger. There is a sense that both spaces are wonderful places to worship, and that the congregation will continue to grow. This has proved to be the case.

The congregation is distinguished by its pastoral care practices. There is a parish nurse, an individual who is a registered nurse, who works with members of the congregation, particularly the elderly and children. Stephen Ministries, a program from the middle west, which involves training lay people to be pastoral visitors. The training requires 25 two-hour sessions, so the commitment is very significant. The congregation has seven active Stephen ministers and three in training. They visit the shut-ins weekly.

The congregation itself is engaged in outreach to the larger community as well. It is a covenant community with Habitat for Humanity for the area. They have a great deal of area youth involvement and individual action. They sponsor the Christian Counseling Center and Family Life Ministry, which began in 1988. They also are involved in Area Congregations Together, a Lower Sabon Valley

Feeding Ministry, as well as The Family Table, a once-a-month ministry to the homeless.

When asked what was most important to this congregation, the building of the new chapel was emphasized over and over. This is not surprising, since it was a multi-year project involving much commitment on the part of both the parish leadership and members of the congregation. The very successful move was completed in 1993, and so a 1995 visit drew a lot of attention to the decision to use the chapel. What is important from the perspective of this study is that the chapel ministry was developed because of a perception on the part of the congregation that they were not doing a good job of evangelism. This very Jesus-centered congregation wanted to be able to reach out to more members of the community and felt that the old and beautiful building, which had been its nave for almost 200 years, was inadequate to this task. Having prayed over a decision about whether to tear it down and build a new structure on that location, and having also considered the possibility of moving the building across the street, something which proved to be impossible, a decision was made to build the chapel. This was done because it was seen as the best way to communicate the good news of Jesus Christ to people who were unchurched and outside of the community.

Christ Church in Johnson has one of the characteristics of a broad-minded congregation: they have active outreach. They also have a clergyperson who is very friendly and welcoming to new members like many of these growing congregations. They have good preaching, and it is Biblically centered. It is, however, clearly a Jesus-focused congregation because of its strong emphasis on evangelism, and the Jesus and Bible-centered focus of virtually everything, from church school, to worship, to preaching, to the decision to build the chapel. While the chapel is indeed the focus of the congregation's life at the moment because so much energy has gone into it, it cannot be over-emphasized that the purpose of building the chapel was evangelical. This is a classic characteristic of the Jesus-focused congregation, and places Christ Church, Johnson, in this group.

St. Paul's, Smithtown

Thirty years ago St. Paul's was growing through con-struction. The building had just gone up and the surrounding town was growing at the same time. The new building provided focus in the early 1960s for the life of the community. The location was a good one; Smithtown was viewed as a bedroom town of middle and upper-middle class persons. Town population growth has con-tinued to be steady, but slow, neither mushrooming nor declining over the 30 year period. The church's growth has paralleled that of the community. In the early 1960s there were approximately 150 persons at worship on a typical Sunday morning, but the budget was tiny, only $7,000 ($32,000 in 1993 dollars). At the present time, there are roughly 190 people at worship, which represents modest growth, but the parish budget itself is approximately $120,000 per year, a fairly dramatic increase. At the begin-ning of the study period, the congregation consisted of many old time residents of Smithtown but contained persons of all ages, and was a real cross section of the town's population, although more highly educated than the community as a whole. The congregation is viewed as having the same profile now.

The biggest change in the congregation over the past 30 years has been its clear identification with a movement known as "renewal." The congregation views itself as being very much Jesus-centered and Jesus-focused. This change began in the mid-1980s when the Rev. C. S. came as rector. She underwent personal renewal and brought the congregation along. She was seen as somewhat abrasive, but a person who could inspire others to follow Jesus. While she was good at selling the Gospel, and there were increases in numbers as well as in faith commitment, her ministry was not without conflict. She rubbed some people the wrong way, and the congregation went through a period of stagnation at the end of her tenure.

The current rector is deeply committed to renewal and keeps Jesus as the focus of the congregation's life. He is also more of a family person, and has a more balanced life. He has brought certain definite strengths to the congregation. The congregation now offers something for everyone, whereas it was viewed in the mid 1980s as having become overly one-dimensional. Now there is a wide selection of programs and a real emphasis on the positive. Prayer chains, a support system of Bible study, and the ability to be "vulnerable to others" is key to this more open congregation. This last characteristic is cited by the interviewees as being a change from the more abrasive period of the Rev. Ms. S. when vulnerability was seen as weakness. The music is considered exceptionally good. An emphasis on praising the Lord is central. In fact, praise music is alternated with more traditional hymns. A time of individual petition with trained prayer ministers begins the 10:00 a.m. service, and this is seen as something which adds to the strength of the congregation.

When asked if there was a time of exceptional vitality,

interviewees cited the period of the late 1980s as a time of vitality as well as a time of special problems. This was the period during which St. Paul's became a "Christ-centered" parish. C. S., the rector at the time, focused on dramatic spiritual change, leading people to focus on Jesus much more than the congregation did previously. This led to a reexamination of the congregation's identity. After a period of two to three years of turmoil, the decision to focus on Jesus was made and held. This decision has continued to be valued by the congregation, and the new rector is a person who self-consciously places Jesus at the center of his life as well. This has enabled people to be zealous but now there is more openness, with space provided for persons who are not as committed to Jesus Christ as Lord and Savior. There is an assumption that over time people will find their path to Jesus. The congregation also has a real emphasis on home Bible studies, with five or six groups meeting together for Bible study each week. This generates a lot of adult education. There is also a time in the Sunday service for lay preaching and lay witnessing, which allows people to testify to Jesus Christ as their personal Lord and Savior. The youth group itself is unusual in that it also has a strong focus on Jesus. There is extensive use of a program known as Emmaus, which is a retreat weekend for teenagers which offers basic teaching on Jesus. Young people are asked to commit themselves to Christ at the end of the weekend. This is seen as very fruitful.

While much of what is cited does not seem to be as dramatically Jesus-focused as Christ Church, Riverton, the worship, described as being Jesus-focused, was not. The parish makes an extensive use of literature. The parish theme, expressed in their brochures, is, "We welcome you to this growing community of Christ." The parish's mission, also in their brochure, is cited as, "We are a Christ-centered community, responding in love and joy to Jesus as Lord and Savior, worshipping together, seeking to know Him through the Word, striving to grow into His likeness, empowered for ministry by the Spirit, extending His kingdom into the world." This is a far more direct statement of a Jesus-focus than would be found in similar brochures from other congregations. The preceding quote is enshrined as the parish vision statement, and can be found in almost every piece of literature which is given out by the parish. The parish recently published a church directory, at the beginning of which is an extensive quote from the Rev. T. W., the current rector. It discusses the fact that early Christians met and worshipped in secret, but now they are called to express Jesus Christ as their Lord and Savior throughout the world, seeking to be faithful through worship, study and action. People are encouraged to become part of this "congregation which seeks to be faithful to Jesus Christ, our Savior and Lord."

St. Paul's, Smithtown, is a classic Jesus-focused congregation, in that the primacy of Jesus Christ as Lord and Savior is expressed as the center of the parish's life in every publication, and in virtually every statement from the interviewees. Some aspects of congregational life, particularly an encouragement of diversity, a change from the parish's extreme Jesus-centeredness of the late 1980s, model broad-minded behavior. However, there is very little question after reading the parish's publications and interviewing these parish leaders, that Jesus forms the center of its common life.

St. John's Church, Transit

In the early 1960s, this congregation averaged about 50 to 60 people on a Sunday morning. The budget was around $13,000 ($60,000 in 1993 dollars) and the membership was under 500. At that time, averages for the diocese were roughly double each of those numbers, and so St. John's would have been viewed as a small congregation. It was a very small church with a very dedicated core and had a familial feeling. During the study period there really have been only two rectors. The first served from 1965 to 1975, and the second served from 1976 to the present. During the first half of the period, the congregation was characterized as being social place with lots of dances, parties, and camping. The rector, who played the piano, brought in a lot of young families. He was "fantastic" at counseling, a real salesperson, and an extrovert, and the church grew during this period of time. One member of the study group said, "He smiled at people, and they came." He viewed church as a business, and the "spiritual aspect" had a low priority. There were no God-talks. This particular rector had terrific personal charisma, was very involved in local events, such as housing for the elderly, the fire department and the ambulance corps. The parish was seen as having much more social life than spiritual life.

Beginning in 1976, Father H. became the rector of the congregation. He was the opposite of the previous rector, strong spiritually, shy, quiet, low-key, never pushes; however, the congregation under his leadership is described as being "blessed by the Holy Spirit." The rector took the congregation "like Jacob's ladder, higher and higher." The congregation utilized outside speakers, "Faith Alive" weekends, a renewal weekend for the entire congregation with a strong emphasis on the Holy Spirit, as well as retreat weekends for individuals like Cursillo and Emmaus, with a strong emphasis on dedication to Jesus Christ as Lord and Savior. Initially, the congregation sent leaders to Christ Church in Riverton to learn what it meant to be a renewed congregation. Over time there has been emphasis on winning youth for Jesus, so the congregation has strong youth ministries as well with a three-year program for instructing youth as well as spontaneous events. The congregation still has fun, and those who like to have fun gravitate to the youth. Others are involved in a great deal of self-exploration. It is interesting that in this Jesus-focused congregation, when self-exploration is described, it is defined as being "open to all viewpoints, all viewpoints centered in Christ." This is a quite different vision from the broad-minded congregations. The congregation now has a budget of approximately $240,000, worship attendance of around 350, and a membership of over 1,000. All of these are approximately double the present Diocesan averages.

The congregation profile is described as continuing to be educated and professional, "as was always the case," reflecting the area in which the congregation is situated. It is also described as having a lively mix, conservatives, liberals, young, old, people who enjoy folk services, people who enjoy more traditional kinds of worship. However, this worship is characterized as being "unified in Christ. All else is on the sidelines." This is also reflected in the congregation's emphasis on "giving our kids a mission to Jesus Christ." Pastoral care is growing, centered in the Holy Spirit and a healing ministry. The congregation is very low-key about stewardship, described as "just a letter and a prayer." The liturgy is characterized as moderate, with healing once a month, but the parish does have a praise chorus. Another sign of the Jesus-focused nature of this congregation is its emphasis on outreach. When asked what they did for outreach, they said, "Quite a lot." When asked specifics, they talked about supporting one of the bishops from Nigeria, having a close link with his African congregation.

When asked to name the strengths of the congregation, the group responded, "This is where people are brought closer to Christ." Love and God are motivations for bringing in more people. "The rector finds people to feed us," and brings in lots of outside speakers. Prayer is seen as the basis of nourishment of the church, and each Monday the staff has two hours of prayer. This dedication to prayer manifests itself in the life of the vestry and in programs. This is reflected in the amount of time spent on prayer in every aspect of the congregation's life.

This emphasis on Jesus and the Holy Spirit has not been without some cost. In the late 1970s, there were conflicts between the "spiritual" and the "social," and during this period of change some left. However, the congregation has more than made up for those losses, drawing in persons committed to the same set of values as the core leadership. When asked why this congregation has grown so dramatically, the interview group said, "Most of it is attributable to the Holy Spirit." "Our reputation is such that people say, 'Oh, you go there?' And people naturally speak of the joy here, and so they come." "We are a witnessing church, associated with Jesus Christ, who is spoken of and made the center of our lives." It is seen as a congregation in which, "People who have given up on a social life, and are looking for something different, will find it here. They will find healing and a different kind of life, and so they are drawn to this congregation." This emphasis on the unique commitment to Jesus Christ, which characterizes St. John's Church in Transit, is at the center of the life of this congregation. It is classically Jesus-focused, with a real emphasis on evangelism. Outreach is defined in terms of winning new souls for Christ, not in terms of social justice or social outreach, as might be common in a broad-minded congregation. Finally, the most convincing proof of this congregation being Jesus-focused is this statement from the rector. "I am open to all viewpoints, all viewpoints that are centered in Christ."

All of the Jesus-focused congregations share four common characteristics. Evangelical in outlook, they reach out to win souls for Christ. They are Jesus-centered, with much "Jesus language" occurring in the interviews. They locate Bible study and prayer at the center of their common life. Finally, good preaching characterizes every single one of the congregations, good preaching being defined as preaching centered in Jesus Christ, in everyday life, and in the Scriptures. All of the congregations in this section fulfill these four criterion which define Jesus-focused, the second largest category of those parishes which we have examined so far. Much more theologically conscious than the typical Episcopal congregation, they are also more theologically conservative, seeking to conserve the precious gift of the Anglican heritage and of basic Christian faith.

CHAPTER SIX

The third path: special purpose congregations

While this study was being conducted, there was a need to evaluate a certain line of inquiry. When the growth scores of the congregations of New Canterbury were computed and ranked it became evident that the parishes of the urban centers had, as a group, suffered the worst declines during the past thirty years. Some argue that people most likely to be Episcopalians moved to the suburbs, and so populations that sustained the church were no longer there in the urban centers. Others just felt that this was due to failed mission strategy and, thus, should be opposed. As a person concerned with societal transformation, which is one term for building up the Kingdom of Christ, I believe there must be some way to support urban congregational life.

Hadaway and Roozen (1995) suggest this path would consist of serving the particular people living in the cities. Oftentimes these would be communities which were unlike most of the parishes in the denomination. After all, the protestant mainstream is largely Caucasian.

This category is labeled the special purpose congregation. Serving specific ethnic or other particular populations, these congregations grow because they serve either growing sub-populations within the community or majority populations under-served by the denomination. Hadaway and Roozen suggest, in addition, that these congregations will be the only ones of the mainstream protestants which will grow in communities with populations of over 100,000.

The city sub-set will contain congregations dominated by one growing ethnic group, often of people of color, Hispanic or African-American. They will represent those people who are upwardly mobile and seek a community in which they can be encouraged and supported as they move out of poverty and into the great American middle class. Few in number, these congregations will be present in any large sample.

When the Growthscores were developed, a particular pattern was noted for congregations in cities with a population greater than 100,000. When the sample was ranked, it was clearly evident these congregations were among those with the greatest decline. In addition, none of the congregations in the top 10% were located in a city with a population of greater than 100,000. This would suggest that such urban congregations may not be able to thrive. However, there was one congregation at the top of the next group, very close to the top group, which was located in such a metropolitan area. This congregation was visited to see if Roozen and Hadaway's suggestion was correct.

Although it is unique, it might represent a general type if a sufficiently large sample were to be obtained.

The notion of growing congregations which serve a particular population niche also supports the inclusion of Visitation, Eaton in this category. This congregation was a mystery having the highest growth in membership of any congregation in the sample, yet not following either the broad-minded or the Jesus-focused approach to congregational life. What was its answer? This special purpose congregation focused on ministry to the elderly during a time when that segment of the population was growing dramatically in the town.

It is important to note that these two congregations were not just riding some population boom. Each had developed a strong spiritual focus rooted in the life situations of its core constituency. They were still following a clear path to deepening the spiritual lives of the members.

The same method of exposition that has been used for broad-minded and Jesus-focused categories is followed here.

Trinity, Leseur

Trinity was described in the early 1960s as being "a melting pot of nationalities." There were many West Indians, but the majority of members were from the southern United States. All were people of color. Perhaps the key element of the early 1960s was that in 1963 the founding rector retired after 30 years. The congregation was composed largely of people who worked in the tobacco industry. These agricultural workers were not able to contribute very much financially, and so the budget was only $10,000 ($46,300 in 1993 dollars) in 1963, even though worship attendance was just below 300, about what it is today.

From 1966 to 1984, the Rev. C., a very strong and dynamic individual, was the rector. The congregation was composed of well educated African-American professionals. The home addresses of the membership changed. Many still lived in the east end of Leseur, but others had moved to the town next door, Deerfield, a community which shifted from 6% to 30% African-American during the study period. Because this particular town has a median household income of $44,000, and an unusually high percentage of Episcopalians, this process led to economic growth for the congregation. There was also a huge West Indian immigration over the last 20 years. Many of these people lived in Leseur's east end, were successful, and hard working, "real contributors," in the words of one member.

The congregation is viewed as having many well-educated, professional people, and lots of outreach ministries that bring people back together. "This church represents African-American leadership in the Episcopal Church," something that mattered a great deal to the congregation. "Trinity is the only place where African-American leadership in the Episcopal Church gathers." While this statement might be disputed by members of other African-American congregations, within the diocese it certainly was believed to be part of the Trinity experience. A major factor in the growth and strength of the congregation is the fact that people who have moved away from the east end of Leseur stay with Trinity. "Even if they have moved away, they come back to worship here." This pattern has continued to the present era and with the present rector.

The strengths of the congregation are several. There is a diversity of attitudes among its people and a tremendous support for children. "I have my biological family, and I have my church family, and if anything happened, I would have someone here to reach out for and to help me." This belief, that individuals are expected to help one another within the congregation, is very strong. There is a sense that all members of the congregation will help each other to move up the economic ladder if necessary.

There is an emphasis on special gifts and ministry and this congregation sees itself as being crucial to stabilizing its neighborhood. Several times the congregation has studied the question of whether it should move east into Deerfield, a suburb in which many people of color reside. A decision was made, instead, to try transforming the neighborhood. This began the "Second Century Project," a project which seeks to raise $80 million in private and public funds to provide affordable housing and housing for the elderly. It is a big push, and one which the congregation believes will involve its best energies for many years to come.

While the role of the clergy is crucial in this congregation, it is not as essential as in some others. The members of the interview committee did say that when there was no priest in charge of the congregation a certain amount of chaos developed, but this is a common problem. However, even with a stable clergyperson in place, one does not hear the kind of clergy-centered focus common to broad-minded and Jesus-focused congregations. The priest is important, but not central. This is also indicated by the response to the question, "Have others provided key leadership?" At Trinity, eight or ten different individuals were cited as having taken key leadership, including the former super-intendent of schools for the city of Leseur and a number of physicians. "People take ministry seriously. The congregation does the work. We take it on and we do it well." The preaching is good, and it is expected to communicate well to the people, but it is not seen as crucial.

In response to the question, "Is there anything I have missed?" the interview committee mentioned the fact that groups of people are crucial to the strength of Trinity. The Girls' Friendly Society, the Youth Choir, and the "Mr. and Mrs." Club, all have been groups that have helped the congregation. The Second Century Fund and Project Advisory Committee has over 40 members, many of whom are members of the congregation. All of this demonstrates that Trinity is a community in motion, dedicated to working within that community.

While it is extremely challenging, there can and will be inner city congregations with solid growth. Anecdotal evidence from the late 1990s suggests that urban growing congregations are not limited just to this type. During the period from 1963-1993, however, they were few and far between. Hadaway and Roozen predicted that those that do grow will be niched, special purpose, congregations. Trinity does superficially fit this description. However, the experience of this congregation suggests that being connected to the community and helping people to move up the economic ladder are also key. It is not just enough to have a congregation of city dwellers, there must also be a spiritually appropriate faith life rooted in the Christian faith, undergirding it. All of this is true of Trinity, the most successful and dynamic of the urban congregations within the diocese.

Visitation, Eaton

The town of Eaton itself has two types of housing, large developments for the elderly, and single family homes. The roads have been enlarged to accommodate the increase in population resulting from the new retirement communities, but outside of the major population centers, a road can quickly go from six lanes to two lanes within a tenth of a mile. The Church of the Visitation itself is on a small, rural piece of property across the street from the big, white clapboard, United Church of Christ congregation. There is a barn in the back, and the church feels very tucked in on its piece of land. It could be five miles away from the town's shopping center, not half a mile.

Thirty years ago Eaton was a small rural community with lots of open land. In 1969 Senior Village arrived, the first and largest of the elderly retirement complexes in the community. This was also when the North-South interstate highway, on the west side of town, was completed. These two events caused big changes in Eaton. Suddenly, there was more money and people in the community. The town more than doubled in size during this thirty-year period of time. Before Senior Village arrived, the congregation at Visitation had intermittent services and was very weak. While previously it had been served by a number of part-time vicars, in 1976 it became able to afford a full-time cleric, and called its current rector.

The composition of the congregation changed along with the town. In the early 1960s, there were very few young families, and no parish house or classrooms. The parish house was build in 1963. Then "Senior Village made this town what it is." The congregation began to prosper and a second floor was added to the classroom building in 1981.

By 1986, according to the interview group, 80% of the congregation was from Senior Village. Yet, the congregation continues to change, in particular adding more young families. In 1995, according to the interviewees, approximately 60% of the worshipping congregation is elderly, 40% from "town." This is because many in Senior Village community are not ambulatory, and therefore only can participate in parish activities by being visited. In addition, Eaton itself is becoming a popular community with families, as it has a very strong school system. All of these are changes in the population, which the congregation views as being crucial to its growth.

While the changing population size and composition of Eaton creates a positive climate for congregational growth, there are congregations that have not grown in similarly positive situations. When asked what the strengths of the congregation were, the interview group responded, "the rector." The rector appeals to a liturgically conservative community concerned about pastoral care. He is absolutely devoted to taking care of individuals. "Private communion to the home-bound, visiting people at home is a crucial part of his work." During the time of the interview, the rector was out visiting three or four different individuals. The parish community itself is also cited as being an important aspect because people are very good about caring for each other. There is "lots of personal outreach," lots of people to people ministry, important in a community in which there are so many elderly. The interviewees did note that there is a minor split between the generations, difficulty in building up the church school, and no youth group at present. The preaching in the congregation is seen as fairly good quality and there is a great feeling of faith. The rector "avoids controversial issues," and can be "sugary." "Theological but not too political," was another comment. Neither stewardship of money, evangelism, nor education was seen as not being particularly superior. However, pastoral care was cited over and over and over again as a source of incredible strength to the congregation. The rector is seen as "absolutely the best." "Can't find a fault," was a generally affirmed comment. "He visits the elderly all the time, has a tremendous amount of spiritual depth, and gives a great deal of time to prayer." "He is a holy person, someone who prays a lot, and also shows his suffering." In the one hour period of time for the interview this care for the elders, given personally by the rector, was cited over and over as being the key to the congregation's growth.

Visitation, Eaton fits in this category because it serves a "special purpose" niche, namely the elderly. The program of the parish centers very much around the elderly involving a tremendous amount of pastoral visitation, preaching and teaching, which fit the elderly lifestyle very well. The community of Eaton, which has an unusually high number of elderly housing complexes, leading to the highest median age in the state according to the 1990 United States Census, mirrors this. Many people retire to Eaton, and as they become frail, need to have more one-on-one contact. The rector of Visitation, Eaton, is well-matched to the introspective and individual lives of the homebound. His temperament is calm, quiet, highly spiritual, and reflective. It is a particular ministry, and not one which would dominate any of the other congregations which have been analyzed in this study. However, it works very well for this particular congregation.

These two Special Purpose congregations share a common commitment to particular populations. Trinity serves the African-American community, while Visitation engages in a powerful ministry to the elderly. In both cases individuals from other groups would be welcome, but this special purpose ministry is at the center of the growth of these congregations.

CHAPTER SEVEN

The other three:
what path to holiness?

The remaining three congregations in our study have been placed in their own category. This is the group in which no particular reason for growth was revealed in either the interview or the demographic data. While it might be easier to eliminate these congregations from the study, I include them for two reasons. First, I hope that some explanation occurs to another reader. Second, I believe that we need to acknowledge that not every congregation will fit into some neat typology. That said, despite the lack of conclusive anecdotal or numerical data, I could not keep myself from offering a possible explanation in the summary of this section.

St. Luke's, Hicksville

In the early 1960s, this congregation had an average worship attendance of 30 and a budget of $2,000 ($9,200 in

1993 dollars), small even for that era. The membership was 130, implying an unusually large number of inactive members. The vicar at that time was seen as fairly charismatic, and saw to the building of the parish hall. There was quite a bit of conflict within the congregation over the thirty-year time period. Some clergy had little following and people left. This changed during the ministry of the Rev. D. B. during the 1980s and early 1990s. This was the period during which the congregation was linked with four others in a regional cluster ministry, served by two full-time and three part-time clergy. Because all five rotated among congregations within the cluster, there was a diversity of preaching styles. This cluster was formed in 1980, approximately 15 years ago.

The strengths of the congregation are listed as having "lots of good humor," "people are flexible and accepting." There are many children in the congregation, and more and more outreach. The parish provides for a local soup kitchen. It also provides shelter for those who are without. The congregation is seen as having a lot of energy. It pulls things together, and there is a great deal of lay participation in the liturgy. This congregation is tolerant of mistakes. The worship service has an ambiance similar to "the comfortable sharing of a family meal." The congregation is spiritually faithful, praying and praising together. Individuals do lots to show care and love for one another, according to those interviewed. This grows out of their bond in Christ. People assume that there will be many differences among the individual members of the congregation, and "make people feel welcome." Currently the congregation has an average worship congregation of over 60, almost more than the building itself can hold. The budget has moved to $38,000, a 1900% increase, one of the largest in the study. The membership itself has grown to over 200, with a far higher percentage attending worship than was the case in 1960. When asked how the congregation had changed over the past 30 years, the group responded that it was more educated, and there are more women now working, which produced some of the "usual volunteer crises" due to two-income families. The congregation views itself as not dependent on the clergy, with lots of leadership coming from all sorts of laity.

The parishes in this category are growing congregations with no obvious characteristics pointing to a particular program or solid mission ministry leading them to their particular growth. This is certainly true in the case of St. Luke's of Hicksville. While most congregations would characterize themselves as friendly, St. Luke's has had exceptional percentage growth, one of the highest ranking congregations within the study group. This may be a statistical artifact, since it was the smallest congregation in the study at the beginning of the study period. Those who were interviewed could not identify any particular reason why the congregation had grown so exceptionally. They were, however, a wonderful and caring group of people and fun to be with. They were interested and interesting. Perhaps it is this quality of character which has drawn so many people to this congregation.

St. John's, Brightfield

In 1960 this congregation was tiny. There were fewer than 45 people regularly in attendance, even though there were two services. The budget was low, around $6,000 ($27,800 in 1993 dollars) per year. The rector was a distant but brilliant scholar who had very little contact with individuals. In 1970, the man who was to be rector for the next 22 years came. The parish was down to approximately 20 people at worship on a Sunday morning when he joined. He was very pastoral and a good visitor, but "a very boring preacher," "kind of a depressing person," who also didn't have very good stewardship skills. He was viewed as very controlling, and there was a big struggle between a long-time senior warden and the rector during the early 1980s.

The congregation has grown much stronger under the present rector, who came in 1993. The growth has been "explosive." The congregation now mirrors the youth of New Leseur, with a tremendous number of people with children with a falling average age. The Sunday worshipping community is well over 150, and the budget is around $90,000 per year, a dramatic increase from the $6,000. The strengths of the congregation is seen as the diversity of its people, who truly like each other. The priest is solid. It is a place which really has a good sense of humor. The church service is seen as loose and easy. If somebody doesn't come to do a particular task, then others step in to take that place. The congregation has problems with poor parking, a very small hall, and getting more than the core group involved in volunteer activities. It is struggling with the change from being a small congregation to a middle size congregation, one with far fewer than 100 members to one with more than 100. The congregation's ways of handling conflicts also have improved. Instead of having conflicts settled by "absolute decree of the rector," there now is lots of discussion. The preaching is viewed as terrific, Biblically centered, meaningful, humorous, relevant to everyday life: "Her sermons can be used the rest of the week." This was said of the Rev. S. M., who came in 1993. Thanksgiving dinner is a key outreach program of the parish, when the congregation fills its hall with people in need. The congregation also believed, according to the interview group, that a 1991 capital funds drive to secure funding for a full time rector helped initiate the recent period of growth. The interview group noted that while the previous rector was an excellent visitor who did a lot with good pastoral care, now, "we pull them in off the street." This was described as the attitude toward evangelism.

When asked if there were any other keys to growth the group had a number of different suggestions. "Christ is very present here," said one member. Another member felt that the recent capital funds drive to renovate the hall was key. Another person said that "the Spirit is becoming more of a reality." Others said that the church people are more committed than they were in the past. All in all, the congregation could not point to any one set of programs or policies to which to attribute its growth.

St. John's in Brightfield is a congregation with good spirit and good feeling; however, it fits here because, unlike the broad-minded, Jesus-focused and special purpose congregations, the lay leaders interviewed could not discern any particular reason why the congregation was growing. Because the current rector came in 1993, the final statistical year of the study period, she cannot be seen as having much influence on the 30 year changes. There was no particular emphasis to which members of the interview group could point. It may be that Brightfield made it into the top group because a small change in the originally small numbers produces a very large Growthscore. As one member of the congregation said, "It took us 150 years to move from 'mission' (that is, a parish needing support from the diocese) to 'parish' status (a congregation which makes all of its own budget on its own)." All in all, St. John's in Brightfield is a growing congregation manifesting many of the characteristics of a broad-minded congregation, but much of its growth predates that. Some of the growth may be demographically driven, but this is clearly not the perception of the congregation itself.

Resurrection, North Conners/Conners

In the early 1960s the congregation was placed on farmland in an underdeveloped area of Conners. There were few houses, and the suburban boom had not yet reached this part of the town. A large bequest of land came to the church in the late 1960s, and the congregation redid the undercroft. Then they kept selling land, piece by piece, to help fund the congregation, exhausting this resource in 1974. During that same period of time, the congregation had relatively few people. It was seen as being underfunded, having a large number of factions, with the wardens seen as "gatekeepers." This particular congregation had the largest amount of clergy turnover in the study, seven clergy in charge during the 30 year period. There were other periods of time in which the church was also "under call," being served by "Sunday-only" clergy. At the present time the congregation sees itself as friendly and loving, "people who will be your friends." It is also perceived as a diverse congregation which has more children than was the case before. It is a congregation which was told several times by the diocese that it should close, but it never did. In fact, the last five to six years have been seen as a time of outstanding vitality under the current rector, B. D. The preaching is seen as very good, "a simple lesson each week." The worship is improving, but "still has some distance to go." In spite of this lack of enthusiasm, the worship attendance has increased from 55 to 121 over the period of this study, and the budget from $5,000 ($23,000 in 1993 dollars) to $107,000. The membership also has increased, making it one of the best growing congregations in the study selection.

The congregation was encouraged to close in the early 1970s, in order to strengthen the two other Episcopal churches within Conners, a town of approximately 25,000 persons. When education, stewardship, evangelism and pastoral care were brought up, no one in the interview group saw these as being particularly or unusually strong. The congregation does feel that it resolves its conflicts much better than it once did, and cites the leadership of the rector as being important. "I wish things didn't depend on leadership, but they do. Better clergy do better, worse don't," was the comment of the current senior warden. When asked if there was anything in particular that I had missed about this particular congregation, the interview group said, "We never quit." They saw their growth as being a result of sheer tenacity. "People love this church and believe it should be here." They are drawn in by the building and stay for the people. Some felt that the Holy Spirit was calling this congregation to be stronger.

Resurrection, Conners, has grown quite dramatically over the 30-year study period. Interviewees did not seem to have any clear picture of why that should be. When the rector was asked similar questions in a follow-up session, he was unable to add any more information or insight. The congregation was severely conflicted for many years, and is currently growing under a happier and, according to the leadership, healthier relationship with their present priest.

It would be difficult to attribute the dramatic growth to this factor alone. Again, the inclusion of this church in the study may be a result of the fact that it started out as one of the smallest congregations in the study. Since the congregations were selected on the basis of percentage increase, this congregation also may be included as a statistical artifact.

These three congregations share no particular program emphasis. The smallest congregations in the sample, their presence may be a statistical artifact resulting from the use of percentage change as the primary measure of growth. However, all cited friendliness as a common characteristic and the worship was informal. While Brightfield may be moving rapidly into a broad-minded growth situation, the other two, while fine congregations, have no identifiable growth-producing characteristics.

CHAPTER EIGHT

Conclusions

I believe that in the stories of these congregations can be found the hand of the Spirit of God moving powerfully in our Church. I have used the admittedly controversial and hard to define word "holiness" to describe the end product of this process for a reason. Person after person in these spiritual communities reported that their lives had been changed. They felt that they had become better servants of God because of the ministry of that particular parish. In some cases that meant serving the poor and homeless, in another building low income housing, in another healing ministry to substance abusers, in another prayer for others. I believe they were becoming holy. Not sanctimonious, not holier-than-thou, but closer to God and better able to live out the Christian values they profess. Light-bearers in a world in which so much darkness seems to be present.

The Diocese of New Canterbury could be almost any diocese in the Episcopal Church. Booming in the 1960s, it has since experienced a long period of decline, igniting a fear that this trend could never be reversed. Indeed, 80% of congregations experienced decline. Some wondered if there was any formula for growth which would work and many different strategies were tried. None seemed to work.

Yet those few congregations which did grow focused on the same basic principles: the purpose of the Church is to help individuals deepen their spiritual lives. Almost by accident, these congregations found ways to thrive by meeting that very important need. The paths were different for each, yet there were enough similarities to recognize some general patterns. Some would seek to follow Jesus, some would seek to follow the more varied path of the Holy Spirit, others would develop a spiritual emphasis rooted in a shared experience. But all would be Anglican, Eucharistically-centered, and led by highly-skilled clergy who delivered sermons that challenged believers while deeply connecting with their lives. The simplicity amidst complexity in this scenario seems to me to be peculiarly Anglican.

In beginning the discussion, a general finding should be noted. The 17 parishes selected for further study had no significant common characteristics in terms of location or parish size. They varied in locale. Some sat on village greens in the center of communities. Others were on side streets and difficult to find. Some were in core cities with populations of over 100,000, others served small municipalities with populations under 10,000. They varied in size, from congregations with fewer than 50 people at worship to some with over 500 at worship on a Sunday morning. They varied in the affluence of the communities in which they were located. Finally, they were different in terms of dominant theological characteristics, some being primarily liberal, the broad-minded's, some conservative, the Jesus-focused congregations. One was ethnic, one "good with the elderly" and some had no outstanding distinguishing theological characteristic.

However, except for three, each congregation was able to articulate a clear sense that the exceptional growth each had experienced was due to the spiritual strength of their particular community of faith, whether through a more broad-minded liberal spirituality, through a more conservative evangelical stance, or through service to a particular ethnic or age group. In every case, it was the perception of the lay leaders that it was spiritual strength which led to congregational strength.

The sociologists continue to argue. Warner (1993), in a paper which has become very influential, argued that an open market economic model is the dominant paradigm for understanding religious change in the United States. In this model, congregations are seen as being in competition with each other for the individual believer, with some "winning" and some "losing" based on numerical growth or decline. Finke and Stark (1992) go further and state that the more demanding conservative bodies better meet the religious needs of individuals, and thus will grow as the more liberal, "low-demand," churches shrink.

Under this scenario the Episcopal Church, as a "liberal" denomination, would be considered doomed. However, two sociologists, Hadaway and Roozen (1995) suggested that there may, in fact, be a path to growth for the "oldline" Protestant churches. They suggested that growing congregations will succeed in spite of more general denominational losses by either following one of three strategies or by benefiting from being located in areas of exceptionally high population growth. Congregations can become either spiritually-oriented liberals, conservative evangelicals, or special purpose. In addition, Hadaway and Roozen suggest that given enough positive population growth, some congregations will grow in even the weakest denominations.

This study supports these suggestions while going much deeper.

The broad-minded congregations are liberal politically, but more importantly they are liberal theologically. "Diversity" is a cherished characteristic of the broad-minded congregations. While social justice and social action are important to these congregations, they are not the foci of their common life. Individual spiritual growth is. These congregations contain Republicans as well as Democrats, and tolerance is a core virtue. This is reflected in the emphasis on the Holy Spirit within the Christian Trinity. Perhaps because the Holy Spirit is less well defined in terms of personhood than the Son or the Father, this spirit-centeredness provides the space needed for all of the members of the congregation to feel welcome. Worship is excellent in these congregations, but the preaching is more often cited as a strong drawing card than the liturgy itself.

There are also growing conservative churches within this sample. These congregations are not following any current "mega-church" model. Rather they are seeking to be self-consciously Jesus-focused within a liberal tradition. This leads to a very real emphasis on the Bible as the center of congregational teaching and education. These congregations also tend to draw members from a wide range of denominations. Unlike the liberal congregations, gaining new members is a central feature of the lives of these communities of faith. Some of the growing congregations within this liberal tradition are conservative, though none are "clones" of the mega-churches.

The two "special purpose" congregations serve two very different constituencies in a similar fashion. Meeting the needs of the primary population niche is the key program consideration for the clergy and leadership of each church. In the case of Trinity, Leseur, this has led to an emphasis on economic development and community empowerment. In the case of Visitation, Eaton, the emphasis has been on pastoral care to the elderly. Both churches have good liturgy and preaching, as perceived by the membership, yet one is more traditional and the other more "ethnic."

The concept that some congregations will grow because they are in areas with growing populations is more problematic. St. Luke's, Hicksville is a high growth congregation in a high population growth area with no special program emphasis. Yet other congregations in areas with higher population growth did not see congregational growth as strong as St. Luke's. The relatively high correlation of population change with Growthscore suggests that positive population change contributes to congregational growth but is not sufficient to be the only cause of congregational strength.

It is important to note that strong clerical leadership, especially in the area of preaching, is a common characteristic of all the broad-minded, Jesus-focused, and special purpose congregations. While preaching styles may vary, they are subjectively perceived as "outstanding" by almost all of those interviewed. Stories about the sermons abound, often quite specific. This reveals an attentiveness to the sermon which might shock many of the clergy.

Good organizational leadership on the part of the

ordained seems also to be necessary for a congregation to grow over time. Their role in making program and educational choices, selecting areas of outreach, and guiding the overall direction of the congregation, is central. The need for a non-anxious and skilled presence in the midst of a changing world is crucial for the growth of most of these congregations.

This leads to an area in which further research would be most useful. The congregational histories suggest that, in many cases, the arrival of a new rector was the crucial factor in initiating a period of congregational growth. Yet, in the Episcopal Church a new rector is chosen by a committee of lay leaders. This selection process might be an area of fruitful research in the future. Does growth come because a group selected the right leader for a congregation or because a dynamic leader chose to lead the congregation in a particular direction? This research model was not designed to answer this question, but, the interview results suggest that further inquiry into this subject is needed. I believe that excellent clerical leadership is essential for congregational growth and that the lay leadership is the group best equipped to decide who is the best clerical leader for a congregation. And let us not forget the action of the Holy Spirit in guiding communities to the right choices. There were times when it seems that the right cleric arrives almost by accident. Perhaps this arrival is the fruit of prayer.

Another finding suggests an area of inquiry for someone interested in the social history of religious communities. A number of the congregations divided the past 30 years into roughly three eras. The first era, roughly from 1963 to 1973, was a period in which there was much focus on "social action." Protesting the war in Vietnam and working for civil rights for people of color were central foci of the lives of these congregations. It was also an era of very high membership for the denomination as a whole. The second period, from 1973 to 1983, was a time of "social life." This was period of progressive dinners, picnics and family camp-outs with emphasis on the community of faith as social gathering. It was also the period in which the denomination as a whole experienced the greatest numerical losses. The final era, that which was most closely tracked by this study, was from 1983-1993 and focused on "spiritual life." This suggests that some congregations have always been sensitive to the desires of the larger social context, and that adaptability may be one of the most crucial characteristics of growing religious communities.

This is a relatively small sample of congregations from a limited geographical area. While it is highly suggestive of directions policy makers might want to recommend to congregations which seek to grow, more congregations would need to be examined before definitive policies could be made. This might prove fruitless in any case. None of the congregations examined in this study paid any particular attention to denominational or diocesan recommendations for congregational life. While minimally compliant with denominational norms and legalities, each congregation sought to find the path which would produce growth while remaining faithful to a call to deepen the spiritual lives of members in a manner which appealed to those who were already present. There was no grand strategy, merely a series of day-to-day decisions, which, over time, created a vibrant and growing congregation. This suggests that leadership development, especially in the areas of preaching and group leadership, and the matching of congregations and clergy is the best intervention that a diocese or denomination can make.

Hadaway and Roozen in *Rerouting the Protestant Mainstream* observe that "churches whose primary concern is making people full of God are also churches whose pews will be full of people" (p.131). This is the case in the vast majority of the congregations examined by this study. At least at the local level, local institutional choices are the keys to growth. While there are two dominant paths to growth within this sample, a larger study might produce more nuances or perhaps even more types. Yet, for those who believe that the shrinking oldline Protestant denominations have contributed in a positive way to the culture and values of the United States, it is affirming to find vital and growing congregations deepening the spiritual lives of their members. The most startling discovery, for some, may be that there is a "liberal" path to congregational growth. The call to follow God can, clearly, take many forms.

The Episcopal Church in the 1990s has turned an important corner. In following up with the diocese of New Canterbury, I am told that 50% of the congregations within the diocese have grown in worship attendance in the past ten years. This is a significant turnaround and one which I hope continues. I love this Church and hope it will continue to be a beacon to many. I believe this research is hope for us all. If we only continue to love one another, while enjoying the diversity and wisdom of the many leaders and congregations of this branch of the Body of Christ, then indeed we will continue to be a blessing to the world in the 21st century.

Appendix 1

Parish questionnaire

This congregation has been characterized as very interesting over the past 30 years. What has happened over that time period?

Thinking back, please describe the congregation in the early to mid-1960s.

How would you describe it now?

How has the congregation changed over the last 30 years? (People, composition, etc.)

Has the area served by the congregation changed over the past 30 years? If so, how?

Has there been any significant changes in other congregations in the area?

What are the strengths of this congregation?

The weaknesses?

How would you describe the clergy leadership over that time period?

Has it varied with different clergy in charge?

Have others provided key leadership?

Has there been a time of outstanding vitality?

A time of special problems?

Could you tell me about resolving a specific conflict?

Has the way you handle conflicts changed?

Is there anything special about your:

Worship?

Preaching?

Liturgy?

Stewardship Practices?

Pastoral Care?

Evangelism?

Education?

Outreach?

Is there anything I have missed?

Appendix 2

Tables

Table 1 lists the "Growthscore" for the study group of 17 congregations.

Table 2 is a summary of the changes in budget, worship attendance and membership for the 17 study congregations.

Table 3 is a summary of the basic socio-demographic information in 1990 for the local communities of the congregations under study.

Table 1
17 Study Congregations Ranked by Growthscore with deciles of component variables.

DECILE: CHANGE IN GROWTH

Growth	# of House- hold members	Wor- ship atten- dance	Bap- tized mem- bers	Budget in $1,000	Score
CONGREGATION					
Trinity, Leseur	7	6	9	10	8
St. John's, Constance	9	10	10	7	9
St. John's, Oldtown	9	10	9	8	9
Christ Church, Johnson	8	10	10	8	9
St. Paul's, Smithtown	9	9	8	10	9
St. Luke's, Hicksville	7	9	10	10	9
St. Claire's, Ridgewood	9	9	10	9	9.25
St. Matthew's, London	9	8	10	10	9.25
Resurrection, Portsmouth	10	10	9	9	9.5
Resurrection, Haven	9	10	9	10	9.5
St. Luke's, Bethlehem	8	10	10	10	9.5
St. John's, Lewes	10	10	10	9	9.75
St. John's, Brightfield	10	10	10	10	10
St. John's, Transit	10	10	10	10	10
Resurrection, Conners	10	10	10	10	10
Visitation, Eaton	10	10	10	10	10
Christ Church, Riverton	10	10	10	10	10

Table 2
Changes in Budget, Worship Attendance and Baptized Membership for the 17 Study Congregations with Diocesan Means (averages)

Congregation	Budget (in thousands)			Membership			Worship Attendance		
	1963	1993	%change	1963	1993	%change	1963	1993	%change
Riverton	15	886	5906%	350	669	91%	213	551	158%
Eaton	3	113	3766%	145	272	87%	52	173	232%
North Conners	5	107	2140%	110	218	98%	55	121	120%
Transit	13	241	1853%	447	1088	143%	125	350	180%
Brightfield	6	87	1450%	159	260	63%	57	157	175%
Lewes	48	470	979%	532	721	35%	167	344	105%
Bethlehem	4	133	3325%	273	558	104%	89	284	219%
Haven	14	219	1564%	504	480	-4%	144	311	115%
Portsmouth	8	82	1025%	115	121	5%	35	116	231%
London	7	96	1371%	263	409	55%	137	149	8%
Ridgewood	58	541	932%	789	1079	36%	325	435	33%
Hicksville	2	38	1900%	138	211	52%	32	61	90%
Smithtown	7	120	1714%	283	270	-5%	153	183	19%
Johnson	18	160	888%	648	878	35%	98	225	129%
Oldtown	16	135	843%	437	476	8%	110	200	82%
Constance	14	104	742%	214	291	36%	90	160	78%
Leseur	10	183	1830%	442	806	82%	350	282	-19%
Diocesan Mean	30	166	553%	768	457	-40%	260	194	-26%

Table 3
Selected Socio-demographic measures, community population and congregational size for 17 study congregations with diocesan means, 1990

Congregation	Median Household Income in thousands	%College Graduates	%African- American	Community Population	Size of Congre- gation*
Riverton	76	48	.3	18,200	L
Eaton	42	28	.6	15,800	M
North Conners	59	28	1.2	32,000	S
Transit	55	45	1.1	11,400	L
Brightfield	43	25	.4	5,700	M
Lewes	58	31	1.1	20,700	L
Bethlehem	29	11	3.9	5,000	S
Haven	59	43	.7	13,900	L
Portsmouth	42	18	1.1	10,400	S
London	42	23	2.5	16,500	M
Ridgewood	69	47	.7	20,900	L
Hicksville	44	23	.8	6,700	VS
Smithtown	51	26	2.8	22,900	M
Johnson	47	19	.7	35,400	M
Oldtown	44	34	.4	8,200	M
Constance	36	14	.5	6,700	M
Leseur	19	4	79.2	137,000	L
Dio of NC	38	20	7.2		

*L = congregations with worship attendance of over 300,
M = between 150 and 300 at worship,
S = between 80 to 150 at worship,
VS = less than 80 at worship.
All figures as reported on Annual Parochial Reports for 1993.

Appendix 3

Change in worship and population

The Demographically Driven Case

It has been said, especially by demographically biased consultants that the only thing which really matters is change in population. If you serve a population which is growing, then the congregation will grow. If your population niche is shrinking, then you will become a smaller congregation. This argument is used to explain why the mostly Caucasian and middle class "mainline" Protestant denominations are growing in the suburbs and for the most part shrinking in the urban centers. Hadaway and Roozen made this argument by stating that one of the categories of growing congregations would be those "in demographic settings where the growth is easy." (1993, p.81)

Hearing this so often that I wanted to see if it were true. The information on the New Canterbury congregations had been organized in many different ways and so I added one more to the mix, hoping that this analysis would help me to see if it was the path of the congregation or its setting which was most important.

To evaluate this hypothesis, that population change is more important than the quality of congregational life, the congregations with more than 50% of membership from one zip code were selected from the larger sample. The change in population from 1960 to 1990 was then computed for those zip code areas contiguous with a municipality because zip codes had not yet come into use in 1960. This sifting produced a group of 84 congregations.

First, a statistical procedure called correlation was done. In this mathematical procedure, the change in population was compared with two other variables, changes in worship attendance and Growthscore(See Table 4). If you are a statistician or a sociologist then the table may have meaning for you. For the rest of my readers let it suffice to say that while a correlation of .302 between population growth and change in worship attendance and of .396 between population growth and overall Growthscore is significant and means that around 30%-40% of the change this hardly means that population growth is "driving the bus."

Table 4
Intercorrelations for Three variables:
Population Change, Change in Worship Attendance, and Growthscore for 84 selected congregations

	Variable		
	Change in Population	Change in Worship Attendance	Growth-Score
Change in Population	1.000	.302**	.396**
Change in Worship Attendance	.302**	1.000	.721**
Growthscore	.396**	.721**	1.000
**=sig <.01 (2-tailed)			

The hypothesis itself states only that some growing congregations will be in places of high population growth. Two congregations ranking in the top 10% of the selected sample were also in the top 10% in terms of Growthscore. One of these Visitation, Eaton, which fits the "Special Purpose" category and the other, St. Luke's, Hicksville was in the group which did not have any obvious reason for high growth. In fact, if you look at the towns with the highest population growth in the diocese and compare their Growthscores, the results are very different.

Below are the top ten towns in population change with the changes in worship attendance and the Growthscores. The "alpha" is my abbreviation of the parish name.

Changes in Worship Attendance, Population and Growthscores, for congregations in zip codes with the top 10% population change

Alpha	%change worship	%change population	Growth-score
STAMDS	-48%	237%	8.75
CHCCAA	115%	225%	5.25
HADCLN	-46%	212%	6.75
VISEAS	187%	201%	10
STPMON	-31%	163%	5.5
STPOXF	-53%	163%	7.25
STLHCK	152%	160%	9
CHCROX	-19%	160%	6
SJNNML	-51%	153%	3.5
CHCRDD	-53%	146%	6.25

As the reader can see, population growth is no guarantee of increase in worship attendance or in overall growth. After all, seven of the ten had declines in worship attendance!

But, some would argue, those towns just grew with the "wrong" sorts of people, wrong being defined as people who would normally not attend an Episcopal Church. So I decided to look at the whole question another way.

Of the 156 congregations in the study, there were seven communities which contained more than one congregation. The total number of parishes in this group was fifteen. I developed a table in which change in worship attendance, change in population and change in Growthscore were compared. If population change was crucial, then the Growthscores would be similar.

That this is not the case can be see by an examination of the cases of seven communities in which more than one congregation was present. The following table shows the Alpha, the change in worship attendance, change in population and the Growthscore for the congregation.

Selected Parishes with change in
Worship Attendance, Population and Growthscores

Parish	cng wor	cng pop	Growthscore
CHCGUL	+135%	+135%	4.75
STJNGL	+129%	+135%	8.5
CHCJNS	+135%	+94%	9
GDSJNS	-56%	+94%	4.75
STAENF	-64%	+37%	2.75
STMENF	-4%	+37%	2
STABLM	+117	+36%	9
STSBLM	-74%	+36%	2
STJBRI	+110%	+33%	7.5
TRIBRI	-70%	+33%	1.5
CHCWHN	-55%	+25%	4
STJWHN	-87%	+25%	1.5
CHCNWT	-43%	-2%	3.5
RESNWT	-52%	-2%	2.75
STLBTH	+204%	-2%	9.5

As can be seen, while the population change is necessarily the same, the changes in worship attendance and the Growthscores vary widely. If population change were the key to congregational strength they should have similar changes. Christ Church, Johnson (CHCJNS) and the Church of the Good Shepherd, Bridgewater (GDSBTR) illustrate this well. Christ Church had a 35% increase in its worship attendance, while Good Shepherd lost more than half. If one chooses the two congregations in Brighton, St. John's (STJBRI) and Trinity (TRIBRI), one had a modest but still positive 10% increase in worship attendance and a Growthscore of 7.5, placing it in top 25% of the sample. The other had a 70% loss in worship attendance with a Growthscore of 1.5, one of the lowest in New Canterbury.

Perhaps the most dramatic example is the three parishes serving the community of Newarth. St. Luke's, Bethlehem is located in the town next door but draws over 70% of its congregants from Newarth. This working class city has been served by three parishes. Oven the past 30 years it has experienced economic decline and population loss. One would expect it to be prime territory for congregation contraction. And this has proved to be the case for two of the three. Yet the third, St. Luke's in Bethlehem, is one of the great growth stories of the diocese. Clearly, even population decline cannot stop a congregation which is on a path to congregational holiness and healing, like St. Luke's.

It has been said that a rising tide lifts all boats. This may be true for some congregations but it is clearly not true for all. Perhaps it only lifts those boats which are floating. Too many Episcopal congregations act like boats which are chained to the bottom and so are swamped when the tide rises.

Appendix 4

The churches under study, pertinent data

Trinity, Leseur

Trinity is located in the east end of Leseur in a quiet neighborhood, across the street from a park which forms the center of the neighborhood's life. It is a fairly modest stucco church in the middle of a block off of one of the main avenues. It is similar in style to many of the churches in the area. It has an attached classroom building and a very small parking lot in the rear. There are stained glass windows in the church and a downstairs church hall, where coffee hour and the parish offices are found. Education takes place in the adjacent classroom wing. There are no lawns, but the grounds are well-maintained, showing obvious pride on the part of the congregation.

Whenever the congregation gathers, especially on a Sunday morning, the quiet vanishes. At the early service, there are over 100 people present for worship. There are almost 200 present at the 10:00 AM service, which is slightly longer, and includes children. Although the average worship attendance has gone down from 350 in 1963 to 282 in 1993, it is still a large congregation by Episcopal Church standards. The congregation itself has seen its budget grow from $10,000 in 1963 ($46,300 in 1993 dollars), to $183,000 today. During the study period its membership almost doubled from 442 to 806. This congregation is thriving and growing in a city neighborhood which is not. Trinity is the most dynamic African-American congregation of the Episcopal Church in the diocese.

The east end of the capitol city of Leseur is seen by many as a study in urban decay. Subject to urban renewal during the 1960s, there are large, vacant lots and many abandoned buildings. It has a small commercial district and parks that are viewed as unsafe at night. But there are also many blocks of well maintained two and three-family homes. This is an area with a fairly low socioeconomic status. Of the two zip codes which serve the area, one had a median household (not per capita) income in 1990 of $13,000 per year. The other zip code, slightly more affluent, had a median household income of $25,000. The area is African-American, 80 to 90% of the population, according to the 1990 census. The level of college education is quite low. It is not an area one would consider fertile ground for a church with such high average economic status as the Episcopal Church. Roof and McKinney (1987) show that the Episcopal Church, with 34% of its members being college graduates in 1985, had the highest percentage of any church in the United States. The Episcopal Church also had the highest median income and the highest percentage of middle and upper-class members. It is remarkable that an Episcopal congregation should prosper in an area where less than 5% of the population, according to the 1990 census statistics, has graduated from college.

At Trinity, Leseur, eight persons gathered to be interviewed for this study, seven of whom were women. The person with the fewest years of membership had been a member for six years. Three had been members for 20 to 25 years, and the remaining four had been members for 30 or more years. Seven of the eight had been life-long Episcopalians, and one of the eight had joined the church after having been a Baptist. Several had been born as members of the congregation. They had been involved in various activities, including the choir and the vestry. Two had been acolyte directors, and many were involved in liturgical assistance. Two had been wardens, two lay readers, and others were members of the Episcopal Church Women as well as past members of The Girls' Friendly Society, an organization for young women in the Episcopal Church. As one member of the group commented after hearing all of their short biographies, "We've done it all."

St. John's, Constance

The southern part of the state is less developed than any other part of the region. In a small town located almost as far south as one can get, there is a small stone church located in the middle of a town green. The church seats about 150 people. It is neo-Gothic, with stained glass windows and a bell tower. It is, in fact, the second structure which serves this particular congregation. The first is a few hundred yards down the road. That building is a square meetinghouse-style structure, which the congregation outgrew in the 1840s. St. John's is surrounded by well-maintained grounds. There are signs in front announcing times of services and adult education classes, clearly available for any who are interested. With the Unitarian congregation across the street and the Baptist church down the street, together they form the center of the small community of Constance.

Constance has a population of about 6,000. It is a largely white community, with only .5% of the community consisting of African-American people. The median household income is $36,000 per year, and 14% of the community are college graduates, a relatively low number for New Canterbury. The community itself is largely blue collar and working class. Residents work at a number of factories located on the nearby interstate. Many others are employed at local colleges and universities and at nearby casinos and a naval base. The community has been described by members of St. John's Church as being in decline but beginning to stabilize after a long period of contraction.

It is not a community which would have been at the top of anyone's list to locate new congregations. But since the church of St. John's has been there almost 200 years, the congregation is committed to staying. It also has grown substantially during the study period from 214 to 291. In 1963 the congregation consisted of 90 persons at Sunday worship. Now the total is typically well over 160. Financially the budget has grown tremendously, from $14,000 in 1963 ($64,800 in 1993 dollars) to $104,000 in 1993.

Eleven persons were gathered to be interviewed, six women and five men. Three of those had been there for more than 20 years, five from ten to 20 years, and three had been with the congregation for less than ten years. Six came from a Roman Catholic background before reception. Three had been Episcopalians their entire lives and two come from other protestant backgrounds. The group had been involved in many leadership positions within the church. Several had served as senior wardens. A number had been involved in leading Bible Study, and others were involved in prayer and healing ministries. Several were worship leaders or lay readers, and some were involved in other aspects of worship ministry and in music.

St. John's, Oldtown

St. John's Church, Oldtown, is a congregation that moved its building in the early 1960s. The diocese had wanted the congregation to merge with Resurrection, Haven, but a small group insisted on a new structure in which the church and parish hall were one building. At the time, the nave and hall were one-quarter mile apart and some felt this was dangerous for the children. The complex now is a beautiful combination of nave connected to a large classroom building. While set one-half mile from the highway intersection which forms the center of the community, it is easy to locate if one is from the community or has directions. The church is traditional wood with stained glass, has a free-standing altar and seats about 200 people. The classroom building is fairly standard, with classrooms for the children and parish offices. The building also contains a pastoral counseling center.

In 1963 the average worship attendance was 110; it was 200 in 1993. The budget has grown from $16,000 ($77,300 in 1993 dollars) to over $135,000. Membership has increased from 437 to 476.

The Oldtown community is a part of Blanton, a suburban community east of the state capitol. With a population of 5,000 it is smaller than other nearby suburbs. It is affluent, with a median 1990 household income of $44,016 and 34.6% of the 1990 population were college graduates. The congregation described itself as attracting the educated and affluent. The town had roughly doubled in population since 1960. During that period Blanton changed from a mill town, dependent on industry, to a largely suburban community dependent on out-of-community occupations.

The lay leaders interviewed varied greatly in their time in the congregation. The longest-serving had been a member 30 years and had served on the original long range planning committee that had decided to move the building. Several in the group had been wardens and most had served on the vestry. Most had been members between ten and 20 years, with the most recent having joined five years ago after looking at other churches and selecting St. John's because of a feeling "that the Holy Spirit is present here." Others had served as youth group leaders, church school teachers, choir members, liturgical assistants and members of various spiritual life groups. There were three men and four women.

Christ Church, Johnson

Christ Episcopal Church sits on a busy traffic island in the middle of the village of Johnson, a section of the larger community of Bridgewater. The cemetery adjacent to the 200-year-old nave completes an old fashioned green in miniature. This classic colonial white clapboard church seats approximately 150. Until recently it was the place of worship for the Christ Church congregation, but the constant stream of traffic between the church building and the parish hall complex across the street with its parking lot, offices and classrooms, created a problem. The crossing was hazardous. Although no one had been killed, the congregation was quite concerned. In response a "chapel" seating 200 was built, attached to the parish hall complex. The new worship space is used for the main or "family" service. It is of simple modern design, with light wood pews and a free-standing altar. All of the buildings are well-maintained and attractive.

Johnson is the affluent section of the old industrial community of Bridgewater. Part of the lower Sabon Valley region, this small city is divided into two distinct areas. The old downtown commercial/industrial area sits by the river. It is densely packed with the under utilized factory space so common to this part of the state. Johnson itself looks more like an upscale suburb with its large lawns surrounding single family dwellings, high-tech industry, and shopping plaza. Because the city as a whole is served by a single zip code, statistics on the two different sections of the town cannot be separated. Yet the entire community reflects economic prosperity, recording a median household income of $47,000 in 1990. The proportion of college graduates is 19%. The community is largely Caucasian with a African-American population of under 1%.

During the time of the study, the congregation has grown. The budget in 1963 was $18,000 ($83,400 in 1993 dollars) and now is $160,000. Membership has increased from 648 in 1963 to 878 in 1993. Worship attendance has more than doubled from 98 to 225 during the same period.

Ten persons were interviewed for the Christ Church study. Two had been members more than 30 years. Both had been life-long Episcopalians and had served on the vestry, youth committees, been part of a renewal weekend in the parish and "done so much I forget." Two had been members between ten and twenty years. Both were life-long members of the Episcopal Church and had also served as wardens, chair of the church women's group, and one had been the church secretary for over a decade. The remaining six had been members less than ten years. All except one were transfers into the Episcopal Church: two from the Roman Catholic church, and one each from the Society of Friends, the United Church of Christ, and the Lutheran Church. They included members of the choir, the vestry and church school teachers. One person noted she was there because "they accept single parents in leadership here." Four were men and six were women.

St. Paul's, Smithtown

In the early 1960s, the Diocese of New Canterbury was finishing a major building program begun in the 1950s. One of the churches built during that time was St. Paul's, Smithtown. An attractive A-frame structure, it is set about 200 yards back from the state highway which runs through the middle of town. Equipped with blond wood pews, the nave seats about 200 persons. The altar is set out from the wall at the south end of the church. Attached to it is a parish hall, surrounded by attractive lawns and a large parking lot. The well kept physical plant contains a few offices, a large parish hall and church classrooms. It is a typical church of medium size.

Smithtown is an affluent suburb of both the larger city of Leseur and the smaller city of Chichester. Many residents of the community are employed in the large industrial plants lining the New Canterbury River, or in the insurance industry centered in Leseur. With a median household income of $51,000 in 1990, it is more affluent than either Johnson or Constance, two communities previously described. Twenty-six percent of the population are college graduates. 3% are African-American. It is a community with a good educational system. Housing primarily consists of single family homes. A new and fairly large shopping district, located in the southern end of town, is believed by some to have been significant in promoting growth.

During the study period, Sunday worship attendance has grown from 150 in 1963 to 183 in 1993. Membership decreased slightly from 283 to 270; however, the median parish in the diocese had lost 45% of its membership during that time. The budget increased from $7,000 ($32,400 in 1993 dollars) to $120,000.

The interview group of St. Paul's, the smallest of all those in the study, consisted of only three persons. Two had been members of the congregation for over 30 years. One was a founding member. One had been a member for 12 years. They had served in many leadership capacities. All three had been wardens. All had served on the vestry. One is a lay preacher. All had been members of the choir, liturgical assistants, and two of the three had been members of the search committee who had selected the present rector. Two were women, the other a man.

St. Luke's, Hicksville

An appealing, small, white structure, St. Luke's sits on one of the back country roads in Hicksville, New Canterbury. Well-maintained, with a small dirt parking lot around the outside, it sits across the street from its modern parish hall. That building contains a number of classrooms, office space, and a medium size parish hall. The nave is a classic white clapboard Colonial style church seating about 80. The signs in front identify the congregation and list service times. It is a pretty church and reflects the pride of its congregation.

Hicksville itself is a small river town in west central

New Canterbury. Reasonably affluent, with a median household income in 1990 of $44,000, it has a high percentage of college graduates, 23%, and is largely Caucasian, with less than 1% of the community being African-American. There are large tracts of undeveloped land, as well as a few farms, and many single-family dwellings. It is part of a regional school district, one of the most highly regarded in the state.

The parish budget increased from $2,000 ($9,300 in 1993 dollars) in 1963 to $38,000 in 1993. Worship attendance almost doubled from 32 to 61. Membership grew from 138 to 211.

At St. Luke's seven persons formed the interview committee. While the congregation is over 100 years old, only one interviewee was a long-term member. Two were members 20 to 25 years, three for 15-20 years, and the last a member for five years. Three were men and four were women. They had been involved in various leadership positions within the church. Four had been senior wardens or mission vice chairs (the equivalent position within a mission congregation). Several had been lay readers or lectors, and all had been members of the vestry. Some had taught church school or had been part of fair committees, while others had worked with children in various capacities. Several had been on the altar guild or buildings and grounds committee. Four of the seven had been Episcopalians their entire lives, two had been Roman Catholics, and the last was a Methodist who had become an Episcopalian 20 years prior.

St. Claire's, Ridgewood

Driving into the center of Ridgewood, a hill town in

the southern exurbs of a metropolitan hub, one encounters a beautiful stone structure off the main street. The entrance framed by white pillars, St. Claire's sits amid a complex of five buildings and might easily be mistaken for a small college or boarding school. Extremely well-maintained, the buildings project security and a sense of pride and accomplishment. This is one of the oldest and most affluent congregations in the diocese.

With a median household income of $68,971 in 1990 it rivals any community in the state. In 1996 a state magazine ranked Ridgewood as the second most desirable community in which to live in the state among towns its size, population 10,000 to 20,000. It is a community of private homes and recently constructed condominium developments. Forty-seven percent of the people in the community—virtually all of the adults in town—are college graduates. In the past 30 years the town experienced dramatic growth in population, from 8,000 in 1960 to 19,000 in 1990.

The parish has grown from 789 to 1079 members during the study period, the budget from $58,000 ($268,500 in 1993 dollars) to $541,000. Worship attendance increased from 325 to 435 on Sunday.

At St. Claire's nine came together for the interview. They brought a wealth of written materials with them: a current parish directory, a short history of the congregation, a book-length hardcover publication from 20 years ago, and the latest "Parish Profile," created to describe the congregation during their search for a new rector. The member of longest standing had been in the congregation for forty-seven years, "since birth." Six of the nine were lifelong Episcopalians, an unusually large number based on the other sets of interviewees for this project. Two of the others had been Lutherans, and one a former Baptist. Average length of membership was 23 years, distributed fairly evenly from ten to forty-seven years. The group included people who had served in virtually every capacity in the congregation including: warden, vestry, altar guild, church school teacher, building committee, search committee, liturgical assistant, lector, outreach committee, hospital and newcomers visitors. There were four men and five women.

St. Matthew's, London

Situated on a side road off the East-West interstate corridor leading to the state capitol is a medium sized A-frame church of modern construction. With no parking to spare on a Sunday morning, worshipers' cars spill onto the lawn and down side streets. The nave is filled many Sundays, with children on laps of their parents. Attached to the church is a small classroom wing and parish hall. On the cover of the bulletin is a prayer: "May the door of this house be wide enough to welcome all who are in need of love and fellowship." It is the home of the people of the Church of St. Matthew the Apostle, London.

Mostly Caucasian with a African-American population of less than 3%, London is a growing suburb of the second largest city in the state. The population has more than tripled from 5,000 to 17,000 from 1950 to 1992. While the number of college graduates is substantial at 23.6% in 1990, many members of the community are skilled blue-collar workers. This is reflected in the median household income of $42,386 for the 1990 census. Housing consists of condominiums and single-family dwellings clustered in classic suburban quarter-acre zoning. It was a good place to locate a new church in 1960, the year the church was founded.

While worship attendance increased only slightly from 137 to 149, the mean diocesan change in worship attendance during the study period declined 33%. The budget grew from $7,000 ($32,400 in 1993 dollars) to $96,000. Membership increased from 263 to 409.

At St. Matthew's the eight members of the interview group had been with the congregation from one to over 30 years. Three had been members since the founding of the congregation. Most had been on the vestry, taught church school or sung in the choir. Unique among the interviewees, they spoke of how delighted they were to be responding to the question, "How did you come to be here?" Six of the eight had been Episcopalians all of their lives, an unusually high percentage, and the other two came from the United Church of Christ. Six of the eight are from London, one is from the neighboring town of Burwell and one from Haven, a town five miles away. There were seven women and one man.

Resurrection, Portsmouth

Resurrection, Portsmouth is a small, white clapboard building that seats 120. Sitting on a secondary highway leading to a power plant several miles down the road, it serves people in the surrounding village. Built in stages from 1787 to 1830, it has undergone many renovations over the years and now has rows of bench-style pews where once there was box-style seating. A separate parish hall, built in 1840, sits next door. The church has existed since the late 1700s and is the offspring of a larger congregation on the southern side of the New Canterbury River which separates the two communities. In 1902 the congregation began a mission on the other side of Portsmouth. The two congregations merged in 1966 which led to a slight increase in size. After years of relative stability, the congregation has grown dramatically in the past few years.

In 1963 an average of 35 attended worship. On a typical Sunday today 116 attend. The budget has increased from $8,000 ($37,000 in 1993 dollars) to $82,000 per year. The number of households has grown from 46 to 130 and membership from 115 to 121, an unusually low number given the household and worship figures.

Resurrection draws parishioners primarily from South Hampton—of which Portsmouth is a village with its own post office. Median household income of $42,752 in 1990 shows it is less affluent than either Haven or Oldtown. 18.2% of the population have graduated from college. People work primarily in manufacturing plants in neighboring communities, at the power plant or in local businesses. The area immediately around the church has larger homes owned by affluent professionals; however, no discrete demographic data for this neighborhood were available.

Eight people gathered to form the interview panel, five women and three men. Four had been members for 25 years or more, having served on the altar guild, vestry, as wardens, church school teachers, youth group leaders, and as part of various parish study groups. One had been a member over 35 years. Two had been members for about 15 years and had also served in various leadership capacities, and two had been members for eight years. Four were former Roman Catholics. Three came from protestant or agnostic backgrounds; only one was a life-long Episcopalian.

Resurrection, Haven

Set on a side road in a residential neighborhood, Resurrection, Haven is a classic newer suburban church, seating about 300. The nave is large and airy, and is separate from the hall, office and classroom wing. There is a large space in the parking lot. The church was constructed in the mid-1960s to replace a smaller building in a neighboring town which had become too small. This earlier building was to be torn down to make way for the widening of a highway in front of it. Haven was viewed as a more economically upscale community with more growth potential and so the congregation relocated there.

The diocese was correct in its prediction. Haven is a growing, affluent suburb of the state capitol. In 1990 it had a population of 11,465, double that of 1960. Haven is home to many middle-management executives and the median household income was $58,819 in 1990. The population is well educated, and 43% of the community are college graduates. It has excellent schools and a major shopping area along Route 4, the state highway which forms the commuting artery into the state capital for many of the towns in the area.

In 1963 the membership was 504, in 1993 it was 480. The budget has grown from $14,000 ($64,800 in 1993 dollars) to $219,000. Worship attendance has increased from 144 to 311.

At Resurrection, Haven the group of 11 persons interviewed for this study averaged over 20 years in the parish. The group had wide experience and included several present and past members of the vestry. Some were liturgical assistants in the congregation, reading lessons and assisting in worship. Others were members of the choir, church school teachers and women's fellowship groups. All were articulate about the history and present state of the congregation. Five were men and six were women.

St. Luke's, Bethlehem

Across a major river from one of the middle-sized cities in the less affluent southern portion of the diocese lies St. Luke's, Bethlehem. The white clapboard exterior is dominated by a square steeple and is somewhat rundown. Though it looks much older, the nave was rebuilt in 1965 following a fire. A large parish house is attached to the church, and a playground is evident. The parking area and grounds are large and well-tended and the exterior offers a distinct feeling of comfort. The inside interior of the church proper is dark wood and traditional, with the altar at the eastern end and seating for 200. The parish hall is modest with a large kitchen. This commercial-quality food preparation area was built with the profits of the very successful fish suppers held each year in the spring, during Lent.

Bethlehem itself is a section of the larger community of Milton. This community of moderately-priced homes had a median household income in 1990 of $29,642, approximately one-half that of Haven. This is not surprising given the lower percentage of college graduates, 11% versus 43% for Haven. The people are mostly working-class and tend to be skilled workers at local defense contractors or work at the casinos nearby. The casinos are a relatively new addition to the local landscape and employ more persons as local industry has been affected by national defense reductions. Bethlehem is a community in transition.

Worship attendance in 1963 was 89, and in 1993 it was

284. The budget grew from $4,000 ($18,500 in 1993 dollars) to $133,000 during the same period and membership went from 273 to 558.

Eight persons from St. Luke's were interviewed as a group for this study. The newest member had attended four years, and the longest standing had been there for 28. Four of the eight had been members 20 years or more, three for ten years or less, and one for 14 years. Three had always been Episcopalians, four had been received from the Roman Catholic Church, and one from the United Church of Christ. Most had served on the vestry, many had taught church school and been liturgical assistants. They had also served on finance, property, and outreach committees. Some had been youth group leaders. There were four men and four women.

St. John's, Lewes

The main building of St. John's, Lewes, is situated at the intersection of two secondary highways a mile from a major North-South interstate. It is a large stone structure consisting of a 500-seat nave and attached office, parish hall and classroom wing. Parking is available in an adjacent generous paved lot, with an additional two acres of undeveloped land available for expansion if needed. The interior of the nave is typical pseudo-gothic with stained glass windows. Children's art and mission notices line the walls of the classroom and administrative wing which also houses a nursery school and parish library. Built in the late 1800s to replace an earlier colonial-era structure, St. John's is a typical big suburban church of its era.

Lewes is affluent, with a median household income in 1990 of $58,363. This was congruent with the high percentage of college graduates, 32%, many of whom are professionals working in the defense and insurance industries. Lewes is considered a "good place to live" with excellent schools. A community of well-tended, suburban single family homes, Lewes is 97% Caucasian.

Membership grew from 532 to 721 during the study period, while the budget increased from $48,000 ($222,000 in 1993 dollars) in 1963 to $470,000 in 1993; worship attendance from 167 to 344.

Six persons were interviewed. Two had been members for over forty years. Three had belonged 25 to 30 years, while the newest member had been there 18 years. Three of the six had converted to the Episcopal Church while the others had been Episcopalians all of their lives. Most had served on the vestry with several having been wardens. Many had taught church school. One or more had served as lector, liturgical assistant, pastoral care visitor, on the finance committee or with the choir. They represented a broad range of experience within the congregation. There were three men and three women.

St. John's, Brightfield

Leaving the state capital, one passes through a ring of suburban malls high-class restaurants and McDonald's. After a while, there is long hill, and on the other side of that hill is the upper end of the Little River valley. Down past the curves and into the flat, one enters a different kind of town, hillier, smaller, with less expensive houses, more sparsely settled, the kind of town where the volunteer fire department is the biggest organization for men. Up the road is a middle-sized church, slightly ornate, white, in the style they call here Carpenter Gothic. It is off the main road behind the small green. This is the skating rink in winter, a nice field of grass in summer. The church is photogenic and appears on TV news as an "atmosphere shot" from time to time. The nave is dark, and there is a tiny parish hall in the basement. The church comprises the total physical structure of the parish. It has no parking lot, there is no office (the office was in the rectory before it was sold in the late 1980's and now is in a rented space next door.) In the narthex, there is literature and many name tags. This is St. John's in Brightfield, a congregation that has seen very dramatic growth over the last 30 years.

Brightfield is actually a subsection of the town of New Leseur, a community that is small, spread out, and hilly. This is a community in which it is very difficult to "get there from here." The population has grown from 3,000 to 5,500 between 1960 and 1990. A reasonably affluent community with a median household income in 1990 of $43,671, it is largely Caucasian; less than one half of 1% of the population is African-American. Twenty-five percent of the population are college graduates. There are many single-family homes. It is very much an upper-middle class community. The people commute to the industrial communities to the north or the insurance offices located to the south. There are working class people in town, and there is concern they will be "driven out" as housing prices increase. It is a fairly typical outer ring community suburb.

Worship attendance at St. John's almost tripled during the study period going from 57 in 1963 to 157 in 1993. The budget increased from $6,000 ($27,800 in 1993 dollars) to $87,000 annually; membership grew from 159 to 260.

Ten persons from St. John's gathered to be interviewed. One had been a member of the congregation for 70 years.

Two were members 30 to 35 years, one for 20 years. Five had been members from ten to 15 years, and one had been a member for five years. Six of the ten were life-long Episcopalians. Three had been received from the Roman Catholic Church, one was a former Presbyterian. Three were former or active wardens. Several had been members of the search committee which selected the new rector two years before the study. Several had taught church school, three were choir members, the church treasurer was present. The 70-year member averred she was only active in the Episcopal church when she "felt like it, which was always." There were four men and six women.

St. John's, Transit

Up the Little River to the east of the city of Leseur and to the north is a large, fertile valley. It is an area of farms and large tracts of land. One of the villages is named Transit. Actually the east most corner of the town of Peake, there is a small commercial district, in which is located a very large, old-fashioned brownstone church. It has a tall steeple and seats about 500. On a Sunday morning, there are cars parked everywhere, not only in the parking lot-which is filled to overflowing-but up and down the side streets which form this small village. Virtually every car belongs to a person who is attending St. John's. Inside, on a Sunday morning, a lively congregation can be found, worshipping in a fairly dark structure with traditional stained glass windows. The altar and choir are at the far end of the church behind a rail, separated from the rest of the congregation. St. John's Church in Transit is a very lively, charismatic congregation within a traditional Gothic building.

Transit is an educated and affluent community, with a

median household income of $55,000 per year. Forty-five percent of those who live in this village are college graduates, approximately 1% of the population are African-American. The village itself is small. The parish draws from a fairly wide area, including the towns of South Grand, Grand and Peake. These communities have median household incomes and college graduation percentages approximately the same as that of Transit. It is an area of expensive single-family homes situated on large lots, some surrounded by horse farms.

In 1963 the congregation listed a membership of 447; in 1993 it reported 1,088 members. The budget has grown from $13,000 ($60,000 in 1993 dollars) to $241,000 during the same period. Worship attendance has increased from 125 to 350.

At St. John's, nine people gathered to be interviewed. They had been members of the congregation for periods ranging from 12 to 75 years. One had been a member for 75 years; five members between 40 to 50 years, and two members for 25 years. One had been a member for 12 years. Seven of the nine had been Episcopalians all their lives and the other two had been Roman Catholics. Several had been wardens, and almost all had served on the vestry. A few were members of the healing community. Two were leaders of Emmaus, a renewal program for teenagers, and six had been members of the choir. Two were members of healing teams. One person was part of a recording equipment ministry in which they taped all of the worship services for shut-ins. This group represented the long-term leadership of the congregation and were able to describe the changes which had taken place during the 30-year study period. There were three men and six women.

Resurrection, Conners/North Conners

Route 25 is a limited-access highway which runs east out of the state's second largest city. The road ends abruptly in a neighborhood of newer suburban developments located in former hay fields. Set fairly far off the main roads is an old, white clapboard church with stained-glass windows and a dirt parking lot behind it. It is a place one needs a map to find and is well maintained and quite beautiful church. The interior of the church has stained-glass windows, a pulpit, lectern and an altar some distance away from the people, beyond the choir seating. The nave seats 100 people and the primarily Caucasian congregation on a Sunday morning includes two or three African-American families. This is Christ Episcopal Church, North Conners, a subsection of the larger town of Conners.

Conners itself is an affluent Westfield County community. Median household income in 1990 was $59,000. Twenty-eight percent of those in the community graduated from college, although there are a large number of highly skilled blue collar workers from the local aircraft and manufacturing plants. The community is 1% African-American. It is an area of almost entirely of single-family homes, with a few strip shopping malls .The community is, by and large, a series of suburban homes, some of them on very large tracts of land. This is particularly true of the homes surrounding Resurrection, North Conners.

Worship attendance has increased from 55 to 121 during the period 1963 to 1993. The budget has grown from $5,000 ($23,000 in 1993 dollars) to $107,000. Membership growth was reported as 110 to 218.

Four people were interviewed for this study, the rector having difficulty assembling enough persons to be interviewed on a Sunday morning. They were three women and a man. All had been members between 25 to 30 years. Three were cradle Episcopalians, and the fourth had come from the Church of the Brethren. Two were former wardens. All had been members of the vestry. Two had been liturgical assistants, one was a member of the choir.

Visitation, Eaton

Interstate 808 is one of two great North-South highways in New Canterbury. It is the western route, with the eastern route (I-860) running along the shoreline. Leaving route 808 at an exit in the northern end of the state, one passes a small shopping area. The state highway is a typical two-lane road with colonial style houses lining both sides of the street. About a half a mile away from the shopping area is a small stone church. It is not particularly well maintained. It has a dirt parking lot. It is dark in color. Attached is a hall of two stories. Functional and solid, it is nothing spectacular. This is the Church of the Visitation, Eaton, the second fastest growing congregation in the study sample.

Eaton has undergone dramatic change during the study period. Its population has tripled, largely due to a tremendous increase in the number of elderly housing communities. Eaton is the capital of multi-level elderly housing in the state, with a median age of 44.2 years, highest in the state. It represents the boom in elder-care communities. It is also one of only ten zip codes that has had an increase in the percentage of Episcopalians over the 30-year study period, from 4% to 5% (this during a time when the average congregation saw a 50% decrease in its market share). The median household income is reasonably high, $41,000 per household in 1990.

Approximately .5% of the community is African-American.

Visitation's membership has grown from 145 to 272. The budget has increased from $3,000 ($13,900 in 1993 dollars) to $113,000 during the same interval. Worship attendance has tripled from 52 to 173.

Nine persons were interviewed at Visitation, two men and seven women, reasonably representative of the proportions within the congregation. One member of the interview group had been there 32 years, one for 20 years, three between ten and 15 years, and the rest had arrived within the last five years. They had served in a variety of capacities: Episcopal Church Women, vestry, Altar Guild, and the parish fair committee. Several had been wardens, and a number were members of the choir. Five of the nine had been Episcopalians their entire lives. One was from the Baptist church, one from Christian Science, one from "nothing," and one from the Roman Catholic Church. Seven of the nine had moved to Eaton following retirement.

Christ Church, Riverton

The early 1960s was a time when many churches built new parishes in the suburbs. In the northern end of the growing suburb of Riverton stands a church with the classic A-frame wooden architecture of that period. Attached to it is a parish house with offices and a large parish hall. Viewed from the road on which it sits, it is unremarkable, except on Sunday when there are cars everywhere: scattered all over the lawn, throughout the parking lot, and lined up a long way in either direction on both sides of the minor highway on which the church itself sits. Over 500 people will attend worship on a typical

Sunday in this church, filling it to overflowing, into the aisles, spilling out into the hallway. This church has been one of the most dramatic growth stories of the last 30 years. It is Christ Church in Riverton, a congregation which started in the late 1950s with 30-50 people at worship, and in its heyday in the early 1980s had grown to a worshipping congregation of over 1,000. The neighborhood in which it is situated is an area of suburban homes, just west of one of the major north-south highways. It is a modest area in an affluent community which serves the larger suburban ring. It does not look like a congregation whose annual budget went from $15,000 ($69,000 in 1993 dollars) in 1963 to $886,000 in the last year of the study period.

Riverton is one of a set of affluent ring suburbs surrounding large and prosperous metropolitan areas. With a 1990 median household income of $76,000 a year it is the most affluent community in the study. The percentage of college graduates in this community is almost 50%. It is largely Caucasian; less than .5% of the residents are minorities. While Christ Church draws from this community, it is also the only parish in this study with a truly regional ministry. When the mailing list of the congregation was analyzed, this congregation drew from more than 30 different communities. Some come from a neighboring state, some from the surrounding county, and others from the counties contiguous to it. While many of these communities are themselves affluent, and much of the congregation consists of educated upper middle-class individuals, it would be overstating the case to say the increase in the budget of this church is due solely to the affluence of the communities which surround it.

References

Ahlstrom, Sydney. 1972. *A Religious History of the American People.* New Haven, CT: Yale University Press.

Bellah, Robert N., Richard Madsen, William M. Sullivan, Ann Swidler, and Steven M. Tipton. 1985. *Habits of the Heart: Individualism and Commitment in American Life.* Berkeley and Los Angeles: University of California Press.

Benson, Peter L., and Carolyn H. Elkin. 1990. *Effective Christian Education: A National Study of Protestant Congregations: A Summary Report on Faith, Loyalty, and Congregational Life.* Minneapolis, MN: Search Institute.

Berger, Peter L. 1969. *The Sacred Canopy: Elements of a Sociological Theory of Religion.* Garden City, NY: Doubleday.

CACI Marketing Systems.1990. *The Sourcebook of Zip Code Demographics, Seventh Edition.* Arlington, VA: CACI Marketing Systems, Inc.

Carroll, Jackson, and Wade Clark Roof. 1993. *Beyond Establishment: Protestant Identity in a Post-Protestant World.* Louisville, KY: Westminster/John Knox Press.

Chaves, Mark, and David E. Cann. 1992. "Regulation, Pluralism, and Religious Market Structure: Explaining Religious Vitality." *Rationality and Society 4* (July): 272-90.

de Tocqueville, Alexis. 1840 (1961). *Democracy in America.* New York: Schocken Books.

Finke, Roger and Rodney Stark. 1992. *The Churching of America, 1776-1990: Winners and Losers in our Religious Economy.* New Brunswick, New Jersey: Rutgers University Press.

Greeley, Andrew M. 1989. *Religious Change in America.* Cambridge. MA: Harvard University Press.

Hadaway, C. Kirk. 1991. "Research Note. From Stability to Growth: A Study of Factors Related to the Statistical Revitalization of Southern Baptist Congregations." *Journal for the Scientific Study of Religion* 30 (2): 181-192.

Hadaway, C. Kirk and David A. Roozen., eds. *Church and Denominational Growth: What does (and does not) cause growth and decline.* Nashville: Abingdon Press.

Halvorson, Peter L. and William M. Newman. 1991. "Regional Patterns of Denominational Growth and Decline." Paper presented at Fall 1991 meeting of New England Religious Discussion Group. Privately Distributed.

Herberg, Will. 1960. *Protestant, Catholic, Jew: An Essay in American Religious Sociology,* 2nd ed. Garden City, NY: Anchor

Hoge, Dean R. and David A. Roozen. 1979. *Understanding Church Growth and Decline.* New York: Pilgrim Press.

Iannaccone, Laurence R. 1991. "The Consequences of Religious Market Structure." *Rationality and Society* 3 (April): 156-77.

Kelley, Dean M. 1972. *Why Conservative Churches are Growing.* San Francisco: Harper & Row.

Kelley, E. Allen, ed. 1995. *The Episcopal Church Annual, 1995.* Wilton, CT: Morehouse Publishing.

McGavran, Donald A. and Winfield C. Arn. 1977. *Ten Steps for Church Growth.* New York: Harper and Row.

McGavran, Donald A., and George G. Hunter III. 1980. *Church Growth: Strategies That Work.* Nashville: Abingdon Press.

McKinney, William J. and Dean R. Hoge. 1983. "Factors in the Growth and Decline of Protestant Churches." *Journal for the Scientific Study of Religion.* 22:51-66

Roof, Wade Clark and William McKinney. 1987. *American Mainline Religion: Its Changing Shape and Future.* New Brunswick: Rutgers University Press.

Roozen, David A. 1979. "The Efficacy of Demographic Theories of Religious Change." Chapter 5 in Dean R. Hoge and David A. Roozen, eds. *Understanding Church Growth and Decline :1950 - 1979.* New York: Pilgrim Press.

Schwab, A. Wayne, Anne Rowthorn and John T. Docker. 1991. *To Seek and to Serve: Congregations in Mission.* Cincinnati: Forward Movement Publications.

Stebinger, Peter A. R. 1990. *Faith, Focus and Leadership: Keys to Excellence in Six Episcopal Churches.* Cincinnati: Forward Movement Publications.

Thompson, Wayne L. 1991. *The ecology of membership change in Presbyterian congregations, 1970-1988.* Storrs, CT: University of Connecticut Ph.D. Thesis

United States Department of Commerce, Bureau of the Census. 1990. *1990 Census of Population: General Population Characteristics.* Washington, DC: U.S. Government Printing Office.

Warner, R. Stephen. 1993. "Work in Progress toward a new Paradigm for the Sociological Study of Religion in the United States." *American Journal of Sociology.* 98: 1044-1093.